Janie declared an apocalypse.

She declared an apocalypse and told me I could pick the music. The leaves were the color of her hair and she stood on top of a mountain of rocks. She was laughing. Her fists were full of stones and she was stuffing them into her pockets.

"So what do you think?" she asks me. Her eyes are two shades brighter than ice, bluer than normal. "Everything needs a good soundtrack, Micah. The apocalypse most of all."

I don't remember what I said.

I don't remember if it happened at all.

AMY ZHANG

GREENWILLOW BOOKS

An Imprint of HarperCollins*Publishers*

This Is Where the World Ends
Copyright © 2016 by Amy Zhang
All rights reserved. No part of this book may be used or reproduced in any manner whatsoever without written permission except in the case of brief quotations embodied in critical articles and reviews. Printed in the United States of America. For information address HarperCollins Children's Books, a division of HarperCollins Publishers, 195 Broadway, New York, NY 10007.
www.epicreads.com

The text of this book is set in 12-point Garamond 3.
Book design by Paul Zakris

Library of Congress Cataloging-in-Publication Data

Names: Zhang, Amy, 1996– author.
Title: This is where the world ends / by Amy Zhang.
Description: First Edition. | New York, NY : Greenwillow Books, an imprint of HarperCollinsPublishers, [2016] | Summary: "Janie and Micah, two lifelong friends, see their relationship tested when Janie is date-raped by the most popular boy in school, and Micah doubts her honesty"— Provided by publisher.
Identifiers: LCCN 2015035885 | ISBN 9780062383044 (hardback) ISBN 9780062383051 (paperback)
Subjects: | CYAC: Friendship—Fiction. | Date rape—Fiction. | BISAC: JUVENILE FICTION / Social Issues / Sexual Abuse. | JUVENILE FICTION / Social Issues / Self-Esteem & Self-Reliance. | JUVENILE FICTION / Social Issues / Emotions & Feelings.
Classification: LCC PZ7.1.Z5 Th 2016 | DDC [Fic]—dc23 LC record available at http://lccn.loc.gov/2015035885
First paperback edition, 2017
17 18 19 20 21 PC/LSCH 10 9 8 7 6 5 4 3 2 1

 GREENWILLOW BOOKS

To the girls with matches in their fists
and fire in their hearts

This

Is

Where

the

World

Ends

PART I
ONCE UPON A TIME

after

Everything ends. This is obvious. This is the easy part. This is what I believe in: the inevitable, the catastrophe, the apocalypse.

What's harder is trying to figure out when it all began to collapse. I would argue that it has always been going to shit, but this is when we finally began to notice:

On the last day of summer before senior year, Janie Vivian moved away. We sat at our desks facing each other through windows thrown open. A bookshelf was balanced between the sills, but she didn't crawl over. She didn't cry, either. She was thinking, hard. That was worse.

"You could always just move in with me," I said. I wasn't quite joking.

She didn't answer. She sat still except for her fingers, which hadn't stopped rubbing her favorite rock from the Metaphor since her parents had told her to pack up her room. Her thumb was black from all the marker ink on it.

The new house was on the other side of town and much bigger. The back was almost entirely windows, and she could see the quarry and the top of the Metaphor from her room. Her grandpa had finally died, which meant that they finally had money again. It was everything her mother wanted. These were the things she had told me in pieces. She rarely talked about it, and I didn't ask. I hadn't seen the new house yet, and I never wanted to.

"It's going to be okay." She said it slowly. Her thumb rubbed circles on the rock, smudging the writing. Behind her, the room was empty. She was leaving the desk and the shelves because her parents had bought her new ones.

Downstairs, her dad shouted her name again.

It was humid. I shifted, and there was sweat on my desk in the shape of my forearms. It had been the hottest day of the year. Janie had said it was a sign.

"This isn't it," she said. She was glaring at me. "I know what you're going to say, and this isn't it."

"I wasn't going to say that," I said. "I was going to say that I'll see you in English tomorrow."

"No, you weren't."

She was right. I wasn't.

"It's just across town," she said, and she was still glaring, but not at me. She was rubbing her thumb raw. "That's nothing. Nothing's going to change, okay? Okay?"

"Yeah," I said, but she wasn't listening.

Her name came again in a singsong. "Jaaaaaaaaanie!"

Her mom. Janie's fist went white.

"It's not really even across town," I said. "Really, it's just down the road."

She reached into her pocket for a new rock, a clean one. She pulled out a marker, scribbled something in tiny letters, and then she opened her top drawer and dropped the rock in. She always did that. She trailed rocks behind her.

She stood. She stared at me. Her hair was frizzing from the heat, and her pockets bulged with stones.

"You and me," she said. "You and me, Micah Carter."

Then she reached for the board between our windows. She pulled it back into her room, and I thought, *This is it.* Our eyes met, and she said, "More than anything," before she banged the window shut between us.

"More than everything," I said, but of course she couldn't hear me. I felt a ripple in the air; the window closing made the only breeze we'd had in days. I blinked, and when I opened my eyes again, she was leaving. Her journal was tucked under her arm and her hair was swinging, and she didn't slam the door as she always did—she closed it with her fingertips, and everything was still. The world had already begun to end.

When I wake up in the hospital and they ask me what happened, that's what I tell them. It's the last thing I remember.

People are here for smoke inhalation and alcohol poisoning. A lot of people have burns. A lot of the burns are bad. At least one person sprained an ankle, and a few people have broken fingers.

That's what the nurses say, but they don't tell me what happened. They just keep saying there was an accident. Every time they leave, Dewey flips off the door. Dewey never fucking leaves. He brought the new Metatron and my Xbox, and he sits there and shoots Nazi zombies at full volume while my head explodes.

"Look, man," he says again. "You were an idiot. That's not an accident. You got too shit-faced and you're goddamn lucky you didn't drown in your own puke."

He's lying. His fingers twitch. Cigarettes strain against his front pocket. The nurse told him he'd have to leave if he tried to smoke in here again.

I feel like shit. The doctors didn't pump my stomach because they were too busy sewing my scalp together, which split open. No one has told me how the hell that happened yet. I'm still nauseous enough to be clutching the bedpan, but the real pain is deeper, somewhere around the place where my brain stem meets my spine. It hurts my eyes when I stare at my phone, but I keep staring. Janie has to text back soon.

"Dude, stop texting and grab a controller." Dewey brought my extra. It's the shitty one that my dog chewed up before he died. "Listen to me. You're keeping the bench warm in T-ball, and she's in the major leagues. You got it?"

Dewey is an asshole. Some people are musicians or dreamers; Dewey is an asshole. He smokes a pack of cigarettes a day and wears his collars popped up and he does shit like play video games with the volume all the way up while you're in the hospital. He's my best friend because we are the only two inhabitants of the ninth circle of social hell. We didn't have options.

"My point is, you're not getting to any bases. You're not in the same league." His voice shakes. His avatar gets filled with bullet holes.

"What?" I ask. "What's wrong?"

Dewey swallows. He won't look at me. He puts the controller down. A nurse comes in. He picks the controller up again.

"How're you doing, love?" she asks as she tries to fluff my pillows.

"Is Janie here?" I ask her. "Is she okay?"

"You just worry about yourself for now, all right?" she

says. Her voice is honey, and I swallow quickly so I don't puke. "Doctor's going to come check you again soon. All right?"

He'll check me everywhere and say things like "selective retrograde amnesia." I'll try not to puke in his direction and splatter his coat anyway.

The nurse checks the IV in my arm before moving away and closing the door.

"Do you know who else is here?" I ask Dewey.

His eyes are fixed on the screen.

"Is Janie here?"

He shoots a Nazi zombie in the head. "I already told you," he says. "No, I don't know who the fuck is here, Micah."

"But weren't you there last night?"

"No, I wasn't. Stop asking me."

Dewey's avatar ducks behind a crumbling wall. His avatar is bleeding from its leg but still walks fine. His supplies are low. The zombies are coming. They surround him. He sighs. "Oh, fuck it."

He jumps out from behind the wall and his avatar fills with bullets. He goes down like a rock. A jingle plays. Game over. World fucked.

"Apocalypse music," I say.

Dewey starts a new game. "What?"

"Nothing," I say. Nothing. I don't know what's coming

out of my mouth. No, wait. It's more vomit. It tastes like vodka I don't remember drinking.

"Shit, man," Dewey says, pausing the game and leaning away. "Jesus. You're disgusting. I fucking told you not to go last night, I—"

He swallows again. "Go back to sleep," he says eventually.

I guess I listen. My eyes are closed, but I don't really remember closing them. Nurses come and go, and doctors, and policemen. I guess I must open my eyes to see them, but I don't remember that either.

Apocalypse music.

Janie declared an apocalypse.

She declared an apocalypse and told me I could pick the music. The leaves were the color of her hair and she stood on top of a mountain of rocks. She was laughing. Her fists were full of stones and she was stuffing them into her pockets.

"So what do you think?" she asks me. Her eyes are two shades brighter than ice, bluer than normal. "Everything needs a good soundtrack, Micah. The apocalypse most of all."

I don't remember what I said.

I don't remember if it happened at all.

The Journal Of Janie Vivian

Once upon a time, a little girl built a house out of Skarpie markers. They were cheaper than the name brand and much more permanent—you had to shed a whole layer of skin to get rid of it. She sat on the floor of her house and drew on her arms until her parents huffed and puffed that markers were for paper, not skin. Besides, they told her, she would get ink poisoning.

So the little girl put her markers in her pocket and went on to build a house of matches. She shook them out of their boxes and watched them burn closer to her finger-tips. She made wishes and blew them out. She stacked them in little rickety stacks and imagined them going up in flames, because she thought it'd be beautiful. She stacked the matches higher and higher until her teachers huffed and puffed that little girls shouldn't

FEAR
NO
MORE

play with dangerous things. Besides, they told her, it was against school rules.

So the little girl put her matches in her pocket and went on to build a house out of rocks. Her parents and her teachers and the whole town huffed and puffed, but no one could knock this house down and no one could keep her away. She named the house of rocks the Metaphor and spent every moment she could there with a boy who never huffed and never puffed. She always kept a marker and a match and at least five rocks in her pocket: the marker to write, the match to wish and burn, and the rock to keep her grounded.

And they all lived happily ever after, probably.

before

When we were seven, I set Micah on fire. Mom always tells the story on our birthday when we blow out the candles together because she thinks it's cute, but it totally isn't because I was making a wish and his hair got in the way and I never got my Skip-It. Lesson learned: bad things happen to good people.

(I mean me, not Micah. He was hardly even burned. And I really, really, *really* wanted a Skip-It. Piper and Carrie and the other girls brought theirs to recess every day even though they weren't supposed to, and I never even got one.)

So, to recap: bad things happen to good people, and that's not fair. Bad things should happen to bad people, like Caleb Matthers.

Cue mustache twirling!

My pockets are full of stones. I drew runes for silence and speed and courage all over my arms and I've wished for luck on two matches. Usually I only light one before ninja missions, but one isn't enough for tonight.

I park my car on the next street over and run through the Gherricks' yard to our old street, and kick over the FOR SALE sign in front of my house before stopping at the door. It's blue, not electric like I'd wanted, but still navy, because we painted it back when my parents acknowledged that I was capable of forming opinions. Not that I'm bitter!

Wait, that isn't even a little bit true. I'm totally bitter. I am brimming with resentment and teen angst.

(And I fucking hate the new house.)

I try my key, but it turns out my parents have already changed the lock. I roll my eyes and hope God will convey the message to my parents, and go to the side of the house. Thankfully, the workmen haven't discovered the loose basement window yet, but it still takes me awhile to coax open the rusted hinges. It's Sneak-Out Route Number Seven, and I don't use it often because of the seasonal spider nest. But you know. Desperate times.

I tumble into the basement and get a face full of carpet, which is still moldy from the flooding last fall. It's all empty—and I go up the stairs and it still smells like the Wonderfully Happy Vivian Family, like scotch and the kind of perfume they spray on supermarket flowers to make them smell brighter than they really do, and dust. I think that's a good way to describe us: our house smelled like dust even before we moved out.

I light a match to get me up the stairs and to my room because the house is all kinds of creepy without furniture, and I wish for perfection before I open the door, so all I smell is smoke. I take a breath and burst through, eyes forward, so that the only things I see are the desk and the window and the bookshelf, and not how empty the room is. I open the window and frown at the screen.

Kicking it out is the most satisfying thing I've ever done.

The noise it makes brings Micah to his window, and the fury that rises in me is sharp and everything, because this is how it should always be. Us, at our two windows, no screen, sneaking out of the house and driving without headlights just to get over here.

"Janie?" he asks. "Um, what? Are you supposed to be in there?"

I ignore that and slide the shelf across and he holds the other end by habit. I get on my knees and somersault over before I can make a better decision. For a second I'm unsteady and crooked and wondering if I will survive a two-story fall, and a second later I'm tumbling into Micah's room and he's saying "Shit!" on repeat and everything, everything is exquisitely funny.

"Oh my god," I gasp through laughing. "Micah Carter, it is an honor to be alive with you."

But he just yawns and starts to fall back into bed, and—*I do not freaking think so.*

So I pounce. I land with my knees on either side of him and he yelps and my hair is in his face and we are tangled in his blankets, and his eyes are the first thing I remember understanding.

For a moment all I want to do is turn off the lights and sleep in a bed with him in it, like we used to when we were little—climbing through the window and falling asleep together. I know the sound of his breathing better than any lullaby in the world.

Instead, I put my knee on his chest and say, "You're welcome."

He is still gasping. "What," he says, "what the *hell* for?"

I push my knee down harder. "For not killing you," I explain. "Benji told me that you can kill someone like this. Jump on their chest and land with your knee, break the sternum, et cetera. I just saved your life."

Benji Arken is going into the navy. He is an asshole. Racist and misogynistic and homophobic, but he is cute, occasionally even funny, and he was a damn good kisser. And he knows how to kill people, which was not why we broke up. We broke up because he didn't shower between basketball practice and when he came to my house.

"Janie," Micah said, and he was looking up at me and his eyes were wide and his pupils were dark and widening, and—

Not yet.

I climb off the bed and drag him up with me. "Come on," I say. "I told you midnight. Why aren't you dressed? Where's your mask?"

"Dude, I have a calc test tomorrow," he says, rubbing his eyes and yawning with too much effort to be genuine.

"*Dude*, I have the same calc test. Stop whining." I throw open his closet and grab our emergency sheet rope (escape route number nine) and one of his (too) many black T-shirts from a wrinkled stack. I toss the T-shirt at his face. He doesn't catch it.

"Where are we going?"

I blink, and I see the scene from his eyes. No, not his eyes. Camera lens. *The Janie and Micah Show.*

Me, standing by the wide, wide window staring at the wide, wide world, eyes closed and arms spread. Him, by the bed, pulling the T-shirt over just his face and tying it into a ninja mask, complaining that it makes his glasses fog over but fingers tapping, because we both knew. We could both feel it. The . . . the suspension. *Something is going to happen.*

Come on, Micah. Let's pretend. Let's pretend, just this one night, that nothing is wrong. That nothing has changed.

Janie and Micah. Micah and Janie.

Can you feel it? I can feel it, like we're swinging and caught at the top of the arc, and we're not falling but our stomachs are. The butterflies are going crazy, reacting a thousand times more violently than they ever will again. They're fluttering up and up, and now they're caught in my ribs and throat and head, and they're so *alive* because they're flirting with something so much more interesting. They're flirting with life itself.

I pull the bookshelf into his room and tie the sheets to his bedpost, and I hold on tight and throw my leg out the window before I whirl around to meet his eyes—*whoosh*, shampoo commercial hair. Eyes glittering, light dimming, and just my voice, siren to sailor: "Come, my fellow ninja. We're going on an adventure."

Exit Janie, end scene.

Except—

"Wait, Micah! *Micah*. We have to take your car. I'm out of gas."

It started small. I think we made a plate of cookies and left them on Michael Wong's front porch because his girlfriend had dumped him on the first day of freshman year. His mom made him throw them out because she thought they might have had pot in them (which obviously they didn't, or I would have kept them for myself), but it was the thought that counted. After that it was cliché: raking someone's leaves, leaving heads-up pennies on the sidewalks by the elementary school, putting an extra quarter in parking meters.

And then: sophomore year. We were stupid and invincible. We thought we were everything, and we started getting adventurous. There was the whole library fiasco, and I guess it snowballed from there. We started wearing masks. We started thinking bigger, brighter, like there was nothing in the world the two of us together couldn't do, and sometimes I still think we were right.

Because we are *freaking badasses.*

We have a hit list, and we are damn creative. We are Justice. We do right, and we reward the deserving. There was the time we sneaked into the petting zoo and protested animal captivity and the time we hid lollipops all over Grant MacFarther's house and the time we hung Christmas ornaments in Jade Bastian's car in July. And there were other nights too. Quiet ones, just us, Micah and me, me and Micah. Swimming in the quarry. Shadow tag in the parking lot by the baby wipe factory.

A reenactment of *Les Mis* in the rain. Stars and stars, night after night, secrets spilled in a world too big for sleep.

Micah is taking forever.

I sit on the hood of his car, and when he finally appears—through the door, what the hell? He knows doors are against the rules—I smack the top of his car and yell, "Driver!"

He only says, "You can't call driver, it's my car. And get off. I just washed it."

"As if you care," I say, but when I climb back onto the ground, he dusts my footprints from the paint. I put my hand in my pocket and squeeze my rocks and wonder if there is a word for the marks you get on your palm when you squeeze something so hard that the skin is on the verge of ripping.

"Micah Carter," I say, and he *does* look up, right at me. And his eyes are the same green-gray-brown that they always have been, and he still has eleven freckles (two on the left cheek, nine on the right), and his glasses are in their perpetual state of sliding down his nose, and this *is* my Micah August Carter. This is the boy who climbed onto his roof when we were five to hear the wind better. This is the boy who, due to a small miscommunication, donated blood during my appendectomy even though he thought it would kill him. This is the boy who is both my impulse control and my very best ideas.

If we can get through tonight, everything will go back to normal. We will be us. He will stop ditching me for Dewey most weekends and I will stop moping in my stupid new house every night. I will drag him into the night, every night. We won't have to worry about going to college and growing apart and forgetting each other in favor of bland significant others, because this is real and always and forever.

He turns away and gets into the driver's seat, and I glare at him for a solid ten seconds before I stomp to the other side. Pick the battles, win the war.

We don't back out of the driveway, we *tear*. His engine shreds the sky. We're going to get caught before we start. "Oh my god, we're going to wake your dad. Micah. I just started my Common App. I don't want to write that I have a felony."

This is a little bit of a lie, which I feel a little bit terrible about. Micah and I swore in fourth grade never to lie to each other about the important things, and maybe lying about starting the Common App is a small thing, but not planning to go to college right away is a much bigger one. I did start *an* application, just less one for college and more one to volunteer in Nepal for women's rights. I want to rebuild orphanages and teach English and sex ed. Not that I know much about rebuilding orphanages or teaching, but I'll figure it out, and I'll hike and take pictures and draw and buy souvenirs in open markets. I'll fill my journal so full of paint and gesso and charcoal and color and Skarpie and words and stories that it won't close. I want to explore. I want to go far, far away.

"Felony?" He sounds annoyed, which makes me annoyed. "Janie, you said this would be fast."

"It will be," I say. "Felony was hyperbolic. If anything, it'll be a misdemeanor, and only if we're caught. I can't believe you're done with college apps. That's ridiculous. They're not due for months. And—turn turn, MICAH, TURN," I scream and the wheels scream and I *think* the mailbox was already on the ground, I don't *think* we knocked it over, but we don't stick around to figure it out. "Okay, next left, second house on your right. Got it?"

"I get it, I'm not an idiot."

"No, *left*, MICAH. Left! LEFT!"

Update: we are not dead, and Micah still doesn't know left from right.

He finally pulls to a stop on the wrong side of the road, and I'm laughing and I can't stop, because, God—

"I miss you," I say, accidentally/not accidentally out loud. Miss, present tense. I'm sitting here and I can still feel distance between us, just folded and crumpled and tangled. Our soul has stretch marks.

Wanted: stretch mark cream for the soul. The stuff that actually works, not the telemarketing crap.

Micah gets all blushy and awkward, but I don't say anything about it because we don't have time. We have a mission tonight. Eyes on the prize. I half kick open the car door—badassery—and jump onto the sidewalk.

Micah gets out too and squints at the house. "Where are we?"

"Carrie Lang's. Come on. I put the helium tank in your trunk already."

"But—how did you get into my car? I finally got the lock fixed."

Oh, please. What a silly question. I pull my lockpick from my back pocket and flash it at him. It was two bucks on Amazon, so of course I got one. I think there's a criminal streak in me. I think it's wide.

But I'm using it for good, see? I'm doing—something. Anything. I'm tired of watching, and waiting, and expecting things to work out. It never works out. It never works unless you demand.

So here I am, demanding.

"Hurry, Micah!"

He's chewing on his lip all uncertain-like, and I tap my

foot on the curb until he sighs and comes to stand next to me.

"Ready?" I ask him.

We pop open the trunk, and I hop in and struggle with the helium tank. Thank god for Party City. Micah sighs, and then he climbs in with me and opens the package of balloons, and when our eyes meet, my smile lights up the entire world.

Carrie Lang is one of my best friends, I think. She called me both times she lost her virginity and if that doesn't constitute a place on the best friend tier, I don't know what does. She is blond and tall and pretty and cartoonishly in love with Caleb Matthers, or at least she will be until she finds out that he cheated on her with Suey Park.

She likes rain and British actors and balloons, and though I can't get her the first two, I am going to fill her yard with the third.

So that's what we do, Micah and I. We sit in the back of his car and fill balloons, and I see us as a photograph, snapped through the back window, zoomed out, long exposure. I don't tell him that Caleb Matthers is the real reason we are really here, that he is cheating on Carrie and I know because Suey Park was wearing his boxers and

I saw them while we were changing for gym.

Caleb is allergic to latex—not, like, *deathly*, but he'll definitely break out in hives. Everywhere. Mwahahaha.

Like I said, the world isn't always fair, and sometimes we have to help it along. Bad things should happen to bad people, but I leave out the details with Micah. I love him more than anything, but our soul is so strained right now that it doesn't make sense to pull it even tauter with unnecessary detail.

It's easier like this, just to be us. It's easier like this to see how beautiful the earth and life and we are. We are stars and the purple-red-blue sky is the background. We are streamers and ribbons tied to trees and balloons that dance in the wind. We are shadows, the too-sharp angle of his nose and the frizzy strands of hair falling into my face. We breathe in the helium and sing show tunes to each other in unrecognizable voices.

"Janie," he says as we finish up, "I missed you too."

after

There is nothing special about Waldo. It is a shitty town in the middle of a shitty state. There's snow for most of the year and corn when there's not. No one ever comes. No one ever leaves.

It is known for having the deepest quarry in Iowa.

It is known for having a nationally ranked wrestling team.

It is known for Janie Vivian.

They take turns telling me. Dewey, the nurses, the doctor, even my dad when he visits for a few minutes between his shifts.

My brain is liquid. They press and press information, but my brain is liquid. They touch the surface and it ripples and then it goes blank again. This is the most frustrating part. I feel it when my brain goes blank, until I forget that too.

What I remember, what they tell me enough times, is this:

There was a party.

There was a bonfire, and it got out of control.

Janie's house burned down.

There were a lot of people at her house when it burned down, because there was a party.

But Janie wasn't one of them.

They don't tell me where she was, though, or where she is.

Or maybe they do.

I don't know.

I sleep a lot. Dewey is usually there when I wake up. He's the one who tells me that my dad is working another shift to pay for the hospital. He's the one who tells me the most about the fire. He must be. He's always there. For a characteristically shitty friend, he's suddenly very dependable. It must be because of the Xbox.

"What happened to Janie?" I ask him. It's a Saturday. I think. I've been in the hospital for a week. My head has stopped hurting enough that I can eat solid food again.

Dewey was leaning forward to shoot, but he flinches and misses. "What?"

"I said, what happened—"

"I heard you," he says, and pauses the game. "You asked what happened."

"Yeah," I say.

"You've never asked that before."

I reply to the ceiling. It is almost white, almost smooth, almost more interesting than the video game Dewey has been playing on repeat because he beat all the levels two days ago. "So answer the goddamn question."

He stares at me. I don't think Dewey has ever really looked at me before. "Usually you just ask where she is."

Where. Where is Janie Vivian. The world tilts; I might fall off the bed. I've stopped puking, but I might start again. I might. "She's gone, isn't she?"

Dewey doesn't say anything.

"So what happened? Where'd she go?"

For a moment it seems like he might tell me the truth; I look at him and he looks at me. His eyes are almost black. Then he looks away and says, "She went away."

"But where?"

"She—she's doing a volunteer trip. In Nepal."

I stare at him. "What?"

"Yeah," he says.

"But why? Why Nepal?"

He shrugs. "She just couldn't be in Waldo anymore, I guess."

"But why didn't she stay and tell me?" The pain is growing. The pain is growing larger.

Dewey meets my eyes again. His eyes are almost black, but not quite. But no, Dewey's eyes are blue. They've always been blue.

But for a moment I thought they were black, the pupils so big that they eclipsed the iris.

The world is nearly sideways.

Dewey presses play again.

The doctor comes later to ask if I'm ready to go.

"Where?" I ask him.

He's balding; his chest hair puffs out from the top of his coat. I don't remember his name yet. He always keeps one hand in his pocket and never stops clicking his pen.

"Home, Micah," he says. His smile is wide and false. "You get to go home."

He checks my head and asks me about my new glasses. I remember that these glasses are new, but not what happened to the old ones. He tells me that I'm doing just fine, and leaves.

Dewey watches the door close. "He's told you that every time."

"Told me what?"

He sighs. "That you're leaving tomorrow, dumbass."

"Oh," I say, and try to remember that. "Okay. But I don't remember how many times he's come."

Dewey snorts and goes back to Metatron. "That's what he said."

On Sunday, Dewey packs up the Xbox.

On Sunday, I am finally allowed to wear normal clothes again. My dad brought them last night, but I was asleep, or I forgot he was here.

On Sunday, the police come.

There are two of them. One is fat and one is less fat. They introduce themselves, but they only do it once, and I forget their names as soon as they say them.

One sits and one stands. They ask Dewey to leave, and he doesn't. His fingers twitch for a cigarette and he remains sitting, so one of the police officers has to stand. He glares at them and asks them why the hell they're here.

"We've talked to everyone from the fire," says the less fat one, who is sitting. "It's just procedure, nothing to worry about."

"He's completely fu—I mean, he's messed up in the head," Dewey says. His hand keeps going to his pocket for a cigarette and coming back empty. "You can't talk to him like this. There's no way this is okay."

"The doctors cleared him," says the fatter one. His voice is low and firm. "It's just a few standard questions, Jonathan."

"That's not my name," Dewey snaps, though it is.

"Dewey, just go," I say. They're hurting my head.

He glares at me. "Shut up, Micah. You don't know what you're saying."

"I know what I'm saying," I say, slowly, so it's not a lie. "I want you to go."

He glares at me for another second, and then stalks out of the room. He has his phone in his hand and he's dialing. I think I hear him say my dad's name before he slams the door behind him.

There's a beat of silence. Then the fatter one says, "How are you feeling, Micah?"

"Not great."

That's probably the best answer I give them. They keep asking questions. If I want water. What I knew about the quarry. Why I was there so often. If I always went with Janie. If she was ever sad. If she ever cried. How well I knew her.

"Better than anyone," I tell them.

The less fat one pulls out a notepad. "Is that right, son?"

He doesn't believe me.

"Better than anyone," I repeat.

The fatter one watches me. "Are you sure about that, Micah? We've talked to just about the entire school, and I don't think anyone would back you up on that."

"Better than anyone."

"They all say that no one ever saw the two of you interact. Ever."

That's true. I remember that. We decided that in middle school. Before that, maybe. I can't really remember, but not because of my head injury. It's just been a long time.

I have been trying to figure it all out while staring at the ceiling, but it's hard because I'm still forgetting. I forget that my dad is working three shifts now to pay for the hospital bills and that's why he's never here. I forget that I am eighteen now. I forget that it's November. I keep trying and trying to remember, but all I can think of is Janie closing her door with her fingertips and the wind from the window and how that was really it.

"It was easier," I tell the policemen.

The less fat detective writes something down. "Why's that?"

I shrug. Shrugging doesn't uncover my ass anymore, because I have a real shirt now. Hah. "You said you talked to everyone at school. Can't you figure it out?"

They watch me. I watch them back. Neither of them have answers.

"What happened?" I ask them.

They don't answer. They just keep asking questions. About that night. About what happened before the bonfire. If I was with her. If I knew she was planning a bonfire. If I know why there was another fire by the quarry. If I drank that night. If I knew beforehand that her parents would be out of town that weekend.

I don't know why they're talking to me at all.

I don't remember.

"Her parents," I repeat when they ask me about them. "Her parents don't like me."

"Why's that?" the less fat one asks again.

"They just don't. Janie's parents. She didn't like them, did you know that? Have you talked to them?"

They nod. Their lips are tight and they do not speak more than they have to. I don't like them. I don't like either of them, but they are going to find out what happened. Because Janie is gone. Janie Vivian is gone.

I repeat this to myself, in my head and out loud, and try to keep breathing as the world keeps tilting sideways. We are nearly upside down.

"Do you know why she went?" I ask them. "Why did she go to Nepal?"

"What?" the less fat one says.

"That's right," the fatter one says. He's giving the other one a look like a warning. "Nepal."

"Why's she there?"

They look at each other, the policemen.

"Why'd her parents let her? They would never let her. What about school?" School. "She's doing her senior project on fairy tales." Out loud, deliberate. Sudden, because that's how the memory comes and goes. Papers by the Metaphor, my voice and hers. Feathers. Scissors. Senior projects. We are seniors, because Janie moved the day before senior year. Her hands with chipping nails, her voice laughing because. Because her parents wanted her to do her project on American economics. Her eyes were pale that day. Her hair was everywhere.

Fairy-tale miracles. And I chose religious apocalypses.

She had laughed when I told her, because we didn't even plan this. We balance the world, accidentally.

And now it's tilting. It's tilting and tilting.

I look up, or down, maybe. The policemen are still watching.

"Her parents are crazy," I say. "They got half the library banned. Did you know that? Sophomore year, I remember all of that. Janie wanted to read *Mrs. Dalloway,* and Virginia Woolf was a lesbian. And they didn't want Janie to become a lesbian. Her uncle's on the school board, and her parents made him ban half the library."

"I remember that," says the less fat one. "A few years ago, right?"

"Sophomore year," I say. "And she crawled into my room one night and we took my dad's car and went to Goodwill. We bought books—she had a list of banned books. She left them in the trunk and the next morning we went to school early and she set up a library in her locker."

I don't tell them how she made me tie a black T-shirt around my face like a ninja mask. I don't tell them how I didn't do much more than watch her. I don't tell them how she looked, her hair falling out onto her shoulders and freckles sharp. I don't tell them how I loved her, how I loved her apocalyptically. I don't tell them how she stole her dad's credit card, or how she took his favorite book from his bedside and burned it while I watched.

It's a good snapshot of us. Representative. Janie, furious and full of ideas. Me, following.

"You drove to Goodwill as sophomores?" asks the police officer.

"Janie drove," I say. "Janie had her permit."

"Right," the fatter one says. He is cautious now, slow. I am talking too fast, using my hands too much. I take a breath while he says, "That's right. It's all right."

The less fat one keeps scribbling.

I might be getting her into trouble.

"Don't tell anyone," I say to them. "Especially not her parents. Especially not her dad. Janie and her dad don't like each other. Does he know about Nepal? He would never let her go to Nepal."

They still do not look at me.

"Who else have you talked to?" I ask them.

The less fat one narrows his eyes. "Just about the whole school, kid."

"The whole school?" That's a lot of people. "Huh."

"But we'd like to talk to you again in particular, Micah," says the bigger one. "And a couple more people too."

"Who?"

"Some of Janie's friends. Piper. Wes, Ander." He watches me too closely. "Did you know them?"

"Not really," I tell them. "Janie likes Ander, so I hate him on principle."

"I should hope she likes him," the bigger one says. He's trying to smile, he's trying to lighten the mood, but we're in a fucking hospital and my head is broken. "They were— they are dating."

"Are they?" No one told me that. Or maybe they did. I shouldn't be surprised. So they're dating—Janie always gets her way.

They do not ask me why I hate Ander on principle, but it's because I am in love with her and always have been. Maybe I already told them. I don't know.

My head hurts.

"I know, kid, and I'm sorry about that. We'll be on our way soon enough," says the less fat one, and sure enough, he's putting his notepad away. I said that out loud; I thought I was getting better about telling the difference. "You just rest up, kid."

"There was a fire," I say suddenly, and they pause on their way to the door. "A bonfire."

"There was," says the fatter one.

My hands. My fingers aren't bandaged. None of me, except my head.

"A lot of people were burned," I say slowly.

They policemen look at each other.

"Am I burned?"

The less fat detective twitches; he wants to reach for the notepad, but the other one stops him. "Were you at the party, Micah?"

"I don't know," I say. I can't, I can't remember.

"Okay, okay, son," the fatter detective says. His voice is calm again. His hands are up. I take a breath. "Get some rest. We'll talk soon."

Waldo doesn't have many parties. There aren't really any colleges around, so no one knows how to throw one. People drink in their basements after prom and blast music in earbuds so their parents won't wake up upstairs. Waldo doesn't have big parties, parties people talk about, parties people go to. Parties everyone goes to.

But Janie did.

There was a party and a bonfire.

There was a party and a bonfire at Janie's new house. I remember, suddenly, as we leave the hospital and the sun hurts my eyes.

The fire was enormous.

I think about this as Dewey drives me home. I thought my dad would have to pick me up, but I'm eighteen. I am an adult. I keep forgetting. I wish I remembered our birthday. Janie must have done something crazy for our eighteenth birthday.

At one point, I ask Dewey why he's doing all this, and he says my dad is paying him. That makes a little more sense, except of course that my dad has no money.

There was a party and a bonfire and the bonfire was enormous.

I repeat that to myself as Dewey bumps along roads that no amount of construction can smooth. They're still trying, though. They're always trying. At the corner of our neighborhood is another tractor laying down pebbles along the shoulders.

Janie loved those pebbles.

She left them anywhere.

I wonder if the police know.

I wonder if I should tell them.

The Journal of Janie Vivian

Once upon a time, a girl and a boy went to the forest without their parents. They walked until they found a tree wide as the sky, a cemetery full of flowers, and best of all, a mountain of stones better than any witch's house of candy, because it was theirs. Back at home, there were parents who told them to fatten up or skinny down, who said that they must save money for school and study and stop believing in fairy world. But at the mountain of stones, it was only the two of them, and that was enough.

Sometimes they got lost. Sometimes they didn't want to be found. But it was a big forest and a bigger world, and whenever they went anywhere without each other, they left trails of stones that led all the way back to each other.

Because they loved each other with the biggest love of all.

Waldo (ish)

before

Ander Cameron is on a ten-phase, month-long, totally *non-creepy* schedule to fall in love with me. I spent two weeks planning us out on pages 158 to 176 of my last journal, and he—bless his beautiful heart—has rushed ahead this morning. Being the most perfect person in all the inhabitable planets in the universe, Ander Cameron has brought me coffee this morning. He didn't have to do that for another week, but god, isn't punctuality hot? (It totally is.)

And it gets better—he did it right! Chocolate hazelnut latte with chocolate whipped cream. He walks into English, slides it down on my desk, flashes those perfectly perfect teeth, and says, "Hey. That's what Piper usually grabs, right?"

One of the perks of being best friends with Piper Blythe is that she lives right next to Starbucks and picks up coffee every morning. But Piper is at an orthodontist appointment today, and I had already steeled myself to the horrible reality of trying to survive today without caffeine, even though I'm still trying to make up the sleep I lost for Carrie, and then—well, hello, Prince freaking Charming.

"You're the best," I tell him, like he doesn't already know, and fluff out my hair in his direction so he can catch a whiff. Lemon raspberry keratin strengthening shampoo and conditioner—I smell like a freaking sunrise. And it works! He leans in, just a little bit, but the little things matter most.

But he, on the other hand, smells like salt and deodorant, which is preferable to, like, no deodorant, I guess. He smells like salt in my head too, just more like the ocean and less like sweat. Alas, life isn't perfect. Who knew?

Here is what you should know about Ander Cameron:
1. His soul is the color of a humid day, when there's just the thinnest layer of clouds hiding the sky. You know there's something behind there—it might be rain or sun or thunder, but you can't quite tell yet.
2. On Tuesday and Thursday afternoons, he goes to the community college and strips—I mean *disrobes*—for the drawing class. Ander isn't beach-boy hot, he's hand-assembled-by-God hot. He's made of the kind of angel

parts that would have had Michelangelo swooning, and he pretends not to know.

3. Okay, so he's kind of a douchebag. That's okay, though. It's high school. Everyone's a douchebag.

The bell rings, and someone nasally comes on the PA and says the pledge, and Mr. Markus does attendance, and Micah and Dewey still aren't here. Mr. Markus sighs when he sees their empty desks (again) and passes a hand over his face. He has time-travel hands, at least twenty years older than the rest of him, wrinkled and veined and knobby, nails like moons. I sketch them on the desk while he talks. (I figure that the no-drawing-on-desks rule mostly applies to penises.)

"The first part of your senior projects is due today," says Mr. Markus. Collective sigh from the class, but not me, because I've talked my way into an extension. We're supposed to write an autobiography, because you have to understand yourself before you can understand anything else.

But my project is multimedia and my autobio is going to document my process—I'm fracturing fairy tales and fracturing them again until they fit my life, and it isn't due until the end of the year. Anyway, Mr. Markus couldn't argue when I told him I knew myself pretty well already.

"As of five minutes ago," he continues, "I've received four. This is pitiful. I want to remind all of you that your senior projects are seventy-five percent of your English grade. Fail this and you won't graduate. Work."

Gideon Markus isn't one to waste words, because he is a genius. A lot of people hate Mr. Markus because he doesn't bullshit them, but I think they also like him for the same reason.

There's a pause, and then a mad rush to the laptop cart, but I just lick the chocolate whipped cream from my coffee and open my journal. Journal Number Twelve feels promising. It's already thick with envelopes and movie stubs and silly things I'll page through and smile at when I'm gray, which is such a relief after the obsessive, writing-only neatness of Number Eleven. Twelve is a good number, heavy with significance: dancing princesses, brothers turned to swans, doors in heaven. (Number Thirteen will be a different story, but we'll burn that bridge when we come to it.)

It's too early in the day to be actually productive, so I pull out a Skarpie and flip through the index of Virginia Woolf quotes at the beginning of Journal Number Twelve to find one to write on my arm. I'm always covered in Virginia Woolf quotes because I'm in love with her. If I could hook up with one person in all of history, I'd pick Virginia in a heartbeat.

I decide on: *Arrange whatever pieces come your way.* I think it fits my senior project pretty well, and that's probably enough work for today. I open Journal Number Twelve to a new page and put the Skarpie to the margin and continue to draw. Planets and universes, fairy tales and girls who arrange the pieces that come to them, and in the center: a star, dissolving, an atom spewing away toward earth with twin souls inside. That's *one* atom, singular, with a spastic and dancing electron field brighter than any sun.

Across the room, Mr. Markus is scolding Wes Bennet for not working, and I steal the words and unravel them until he's narrating in his sandpaper voice.

Once upon a time, he says, and I draw in furious little strokes, *in the beginning, there was no such thing as darkness. There were only stars bridged by light, and a single atom with wings.*

Wings—they're going to be my masterpiece. They're going to blow everyone away, out of the water, into oblivion. Good-bye, Wes Bennet and your fuck-the-system paper on American education. So long, Piper Blythe and your (admittedly really cool) thesis on cognitive biases and human failure. Even you, Micah, and your apocalypses. My wings are going to put you all to shame.

I start sketching again: wire for the frame, canvas over bamboo, feathers cut from Andersen and Grimm.

Fairy-tale monster wings, shaped like butterfly but feathered like bird, clawed like bat and wider than dragon.

Then the Skarpie lines trail and jerk, learning to fly. They morph into birds and trees and veins and dreamers and a few rabid scribble creatures that snarl at the idea of being mistakes. There. I have one wing stretching and another that collapses into the whole wide world.

Mr. Markus almost didn't agree to my proposal. I wheedled and begged and bribed (with cookies) the yes out of him. He says my problem is that I was born with a thousand beginnings and no endings at all. It's hard to argue with that, because there's an awful lot of proof in the senior studio art room. Projects upon unfinished projects: a teapot with no lid, four saucers and one teacup, a clay map of the world minus Australia, seven or eight untrimmed bowls, one ball of wedged clay that I lost and found after it fossilized and covered in Viking runes for luck.

Not this time, though. I will finish the wings if it kills me. I will! You'll see.

The door bursts open. Dewey struts in with his stupid collar to his chin and Micah trails in behind him with cartoonishly bad bedhead and caffeine in his fingers. You see guys doing the air piano thing all the time, tapping their fingers on the edges of the desk while they sit sprawled in the chair with their legs wide open, thinking they're so *cool*. Micah doesn't do that. Micah is all nervous habit and music that never goes away.

Mr. Markus barely spares them a glance. "Sit down," he says, and then goes back to typing. That's another thing about Mr. Markus—he does all of our projects with us. He doesn't just sit on the computer with the screen turned away so he can grade papers or play games or watch porn.

Micah ducks his head and slides into a desk while Dewey mutters something about how it's not his fault that Micah drives a piece of shit. Micah catches me licking whipped cream off my finger and smiles, but I have to ignore him because right then—

"Hey," Ander whispers. He leans over, and his angel smile makes me feel just right: quirky but not hipster, talented but not cocky, sunshine without the burn. "I like those shoes on you."

Such adorable bullshit. Ander is the worst flirt in the world, and he has no idea at all. Being with him is like riding a hot air balloon inflated by his ego—the view is great, the heat is everywhere. I don't know why I like him, just that I do, and that's okay. It is! People say *because* too much. You don't always need a reason. I want cliché and simple. I want Journal Number Twelve to be heat and moments. Condensation gathering on Starbucks cups with my name spelled wrong. White people almost kissing. Boyfriend in plaid. Hot dog legs and sunshine.

Ander leans a bit more. This is important, the leaning, because it makes my heart beat so hard it feels like it's going to break a rib. If I die of a heart attack or something one day (GOD FORBID—I will not die of something boring, I *won't*), it will have been caused by this moment. The corners of his mouth quirk and he shows his gorgeous teeth again, and my insides go all soft because our babies would be the most perfect babies in the history of ever.

"Hey," he says again, catching sight of my sketches. He pushes my hand back to look at the scribbles, the universes and wings and stars, and I freeze. "That's really pretty. Needs a rocket ship, though. Vroom."

No. You don't get to look, angel boy. You don't get to push my hand aside.

But I don't snatch it away. I swallow and I—

What do I do?

I add a rocket ship. *I add a goddamn rocket ship.*

(Side note: did he say *vroom*?)

"Now go write your paper," I say, bumping my shoulder against his. Not even to touch him—okay, a little bit to touch him—but to angle myself away.

But aren't boyfriends—would be, will be—supposed to be like this? Peeking over your shoulder and grinning their lopsided grins, faking interest in your stupid little scribbles. I wanted this so badly when I was dating Jeff Martin, who only ever wanted to make out, which would have been fine if he didn't nibble so much.

"Mr. Carter," Mr. Markus says sharply. "Why bother coming to class at all? You show up late, and you make no effort at all to even pretend to work. Your classmates, at least, give that much. I can only assume that you're finished with your paper, as you and Mr. Dewey seem far more preoccupied by rubber bands than your education."

Micah's head snaps up. His entire head this time, not just his eyes, and it looks painful. Everything Micah does looks painful. He moves too quickly, and everything looks like a flinch. I can't decide if Micah is cute or not, but once I heard a couple of sophomores saying that he has bedroom eyes.

Not that I was jealous or anything.

It's just that—well, we had already drawn lines on our soul and stabbed our little flags into it. We had claimed. Him: music and reality and all the words too shy to be spoken. Me: art and dreams in Technicolor and everything that had ever happened in sunshine and all the secrets exchanged in moonlight. We agreed on all of that before even the dinosaurs stomped around, and he isn't *allowed* to change that now.

And it's not like *they* noticed before. Before his acne

cleared up and the barber gave him that undercut (which I maintain is really a Hitler Youth haircut) and hipster glasses were suddenly in. *I* did. *I* always knew that his best feature was his eyelashes. And that his glasses prescription is wrong, so when he's squinting and his eyelashes get all tangled and he does that rapid fluttery blinking thing, it's because he can't see, not because he *understands* you, stupid little sophomores.

But anyway.

"Um," says Micah. His rubber-band gun drops onto his desk.

Next to him, Dewey mutters, "Yeah, rubber bands trump this shithole."

"Fantastic," says Mr. Markus, leaning back in his chair and motioning for Micah to go to the podium in the front. "Then, please. Read us your papers. We'll have group critique."

Dewey claps Micah on the shoulder. "All you, man."

I can see Micah swallow from across the room.

It takes him an eternity, two, to make his way to the front. His throat clenches and his paper wrinkles in his hands, and someone giggles. I glare in the general direction. My glare razes—I've spent too long perfecting it in the mirror for it not to. Kelsey Davenport quivers.

The razing is okay. It's politeness, really, to make sure

no one makes fun of Micah. We're very good about our interaction now, in school. Seventh grade was the hardest, when I got boobs and he got pimples, and we needed each other more than anything but couldn't even talk in school because I thought I was too cool. But it really is better this way. I think. It's easier for both of us to have our own friends at school and not try to combine them, but maybe a little easier for me than for him.

"If there is one thing that science and religion agree on," he begins, stutters, coughs, clears his throat. "If there is one thing that science and religion agree on, it's the fact that the world is going to end. Maybe the sun will go out or God will rain his wrath down or a giant wolf will swallow the earth whole, but throughout it all is the pervasive idea of entropy. It's all unraveling. Everything is stumbling toward an ending."

Ander coughs. His lips are twitching, and he catches Wes Bennet's eye, and they exchange their jock-y smirks. (Sigh. I have a massive crush on an asshole. How cliché.) Micah is bright red, and he does his head-duck thing, where he pulls his shoulders to his ears and doesn't know where to look.

Micah lives like an apology. He blushes when he breathes because he's taking someone else's air. It's like all Micah wants is to disappear, and he thinks if he's quiet enough, if he keeps his eyes on the ground and barely breathes and treads lightly, people will forget he exists.

But he has it all wrong. Here is how you disappear: you dive into your DNA and rip out everything but carbon. You copy. Carbon copy—see what I did there? And then you keep going. You apply to college because you're supposed to and then you complain about debt and the classes and the whole system because that's what everyone else does. You run into businessmen in untailored suits and you marry the lamest one and you move into a nice picture-perfect house full of clock hands that point at the cemetery. Don't worry. The tide will sweep you right up.

I stare at him, hard, and tug on our soul until he looks at me.

"More than anything," I mouth to him since no one is looking, and his shoulders relax. He smiles. His eyes and my eyes—our soul is so bright.

Oh, Micah. I'll never let the tide take us.

But then Ander glances over again and gives me a flashing side grin, there and gone, and I know I'm sitting at a desk and everything, but still—my knees go Jell-O weak.

after

They meant it. The police, I mean. They meant it when they said that we would talk soon. They ask me about everything. Everything. They ask me about Janie, and that is the same thing.

They tell me about the fire.

They tell me that they think someone set it.

"Yes," I say. "It was a bonfire. Wasn't it?"

Yes, they say, impatient. I imagine because they've said it before. Yes, it was a bonfire. But the bonfire spread. Someone probably made it spread.

"Who?" I ask.

They tell me there was gasoline.

They tell me that it was everywhere, but especially the second floor. Especially her room.

They ask me if I knew that Janie and I spent that entire night together. They ask me why that was, since we didn't

49

want anyone to know we were friends. They ask me again why that was.

The truth is I don't know how to answer. She is Janie Vivian, and I am Micah Carter. I don't know how to explain it further than that.

Dewey is still babysitting. After the police leave, I go down to the basement and find him playing Metatron again.

"You gotta just stop talking to those assholes," he says when he sees me. "Your dad told me to tell you not to say anything else to them unless they get a search warrant or something."

I ignore that, because my dad can tell me himself if he ever decides to come home. Where is he again? I don't care enough to ask. "I want to see her house," I say.

Dewey plays Metatron with his entire body. He ducks a bullet and a zombie bite and lunges forward to shoot. "Nothing to see," he says, and ducks again. He hits his head on the edge of the coffee table. "Oh, *fuck*." He pauses the game to glare at me like it's my fault. "Will you grab a fucking controller already?"

"Will you drive?" My license is suspended until further notice. I'm almost able to walk in a straight line, though, so the reinstatement is within sight.

"Why the fuck would I do that?"

"I'm going either way," I say. "I just don't want to walk."

It's cold, which is weird. I keep walking outside in shorts because I'm still expecting September. But of course it isn't September.

"Give me a sec," Dewey says, and starts the game over.

I start back up the stairs.

"All right—all right! I'm coming. Dammit, Micah."

We head toward the quarry. They're doing construction on the roads. There's gravel on the shoulders to prepare for the tar, and I keep looking at it. I don't know why.

I mention this to Dewey and he tells me that I already know this, and I remember that I do. I think this is a good sign.

It is cloudy today. It is the kind of cloudy that makes everything look colorless. I think about her eyes.

Dewey drives and I check my phone. Janie has not texted me back. I have sent her a text every morning at 7:31, but she has not texted back.

Dewey is a worse driver sober than drunk. He takes the turn into Waldo's only nice neighborhood, opposite the turn into the quarry, but he takes it sloppily and swerves into the sidewalk just as someone passes.

He almost kills her but doesn't, and as Dewey swears and honks, I twist in my seat.

"That's Piper," I say, but she doesn't even stop to flip us off. She's already going. Gone. "She was crying."

Dewey reverses and gets the car back onto the road. "She wasn't crying."

"Why was she crying?"

"She wasn't fucking crying," Dewey says. He doesn't look at me.

We drive in silence.

The trees here are tall, the houses are nearly taller. They look obscene and hollow. The shutters are fake, and the houses are too far apart to climb from window to window. It's a new development and most of the houses are empty, because no one in Waldo has the money to live here. Of course Janie hated it.

Dewey turns again, and I see it. He's right. There's nothing left to see. Except the black toothpick frame of the house. The beams poke out of the ground like the ribs of a giant. They remind me of Janie's fairy tales. Nothing else is black. They don't tell you that about fires. I thought it would all be burned black, but it's not. Everything is gray. It is all the same color as the sky.

I am out of the car, but I don't remember unbuckling my seat belt. Or opening the door. But I am outside and it's dry and it still smells like fire.

The grass is crisp under my feet.

"Micah, don't," I hear Dewey say.

There is yellow tape everywhere, but I duck under. I ignore Dewey, and he doesn't come after me.

The world is tilting, but I still don't remember.

The sun is hidden, but it still hurts my eyes.

And my lungs.

Among the toothpicks is half an armchair. The chimney and the fireplace. Something that might have been a piano. I don't remember the armchair. They must have gotten it after they moved. That's right. I remember Janie talking about the new furniture, and hating that too.

"Micah?"

I flinch, and turn to see Mr. Vivian standing at the end of the driveway, and Dewey diving back into the car to avoid whatever is going to happen next. Janie's dad is a big man, but he looks gray too. He used to be on the football team at Waldo High, and the track team. He used to date Piper's mom, and also Wes Bennet's mom, and they might have overlapped. Janie told me that freshman year. She was convinced her parents could have been happy with anyone but each other.

"Isn't that funny?" she had said. We had just come back from a ninja mission. She was perched on the windowsill, about to climb away. "If there's one person in the world you should be with, there must be one person in the world you shouldn't be with. Well, I mean, a lot of people. But one person in particular. Don't you think it's funny that out of all the people in the whole wide world, my parents ended up with each other? I do."

It's not a helpful memory. It's not what I came here to remember.

"Micah, what are you doing here?" asks Mr. Vivian. He walks up the driveway slowly but doesn't cross the yellow tape.

I watch him but keep walking backward. The ash is thickening. It reaches my ankles. It covers my shoes. I look up; the sky is the same color as the ground. "Is this where her room used to be?" I ask him.

His jaw is tight.

I look around. The trees are fine, mostly. Some of the branches are burned, but for the most part, they're okay. They cage the house in.

"She lied," I said. "You can't see the Metaphor from here."

"Micah, you know you can't be here," he calls. "It's blocked off for a reason. And you—you especially can't be here."

He's almost yelling. He says *you* like it's shit in his mouth.

"Will you move back now?" I ask.

There is a screw in his jawbone and it's tightening and the tension is too much.

"Leave," he tells me, and I wish—I wish I could. But my feet have sunk into the ash. I can only look at him. His eyes are bluer than Janie's. His hair is dark, but his beard is red like her hair. I can see Janie in him. I would never tell her that. She would never listen. She would probably punch me if I said it. But I can see her in him.

"Micah," he says. "I want you off my property. I want you to leave. I never want you near my family again. I don't ever want to find you here again. The next time I want to see you is in court."

You can see the quarry from here, so that part was true. But I can't see the Metaphor. There's Old Eell's barn and so I should be able to see the Metaphor, and Janie wouldn't lie about that. Janie would never lie about the Metaphor.

"I have to go," I say, and I stumble past him and down the driveway, where Dewey is waiting in his car. I don't remember when he did that. He must have dived in when he saw Mr. Vivian, which doesn't surprise me. Dewey usually solves problems by getting the fuck out of there.

I am still walking toward Dewey's car, I am still staring at my best friend who is an asshole safe inside, I am still wondering why I couldn't see the Metaphor from the top of the hill.

But then suddenly I am also in my bed, and the room is

dark, and Janie is beside me. We are tangled in the blankets. Her head is in my pillow and she is screaming. Her father is standing in the door, and he fills the room.

The moment fractures and turns to dust. Ash.

I stumble into the car.

"Let's drive to the quarry," I tell Dewey, and he does.

In the car, I remember again. "What did Janie's dad mean, about court? And me?"

Dewey hauls ass towards the quarry, away from the tall, empty houses. "He didn't mean anything."

"You didn't even hear."

"So why the fuck are you asking me, then?"

"Because you're not telling me something," I say, and his hands tighten on the steering wheel. "My dad too. He always says he's too tired to talk when I ask him. What's going on?"

"Nothing," he says, taking a turn that throws me against the door. "Nothing's going on. Keep your damn mouth shut and nothing's going to happen. If you don't remember it, don't fucking talk about it. That's it. It's easy."

"What's easy?"

The road is now gravel. Pebbles. "Dammit, Micah. What the hell do you think? Use your stupid busted head. Why the hell do you think the police have been around so much? Why do you think they keep wanting to talk about the fire?"

When he puts it like that, the answer is obvious.

They think I set it.

Dewey slows to a stop by the edge of the quarry.

The deepest part of the quarry is two hundred and nineteen feet deep. The water rarely gets warmer than fifty degrees in the dead of summer. This used to be the greatest limestone mine in the northern Midwest, which is hard to imagine. It's hard to imagine anything under the water. It's too dark.

The quarry is blocked off by a chain fence that is never closed. There is a NO TRESPASSING sign that is missing most of its letters. On the far side, there is a ledge where stoners dare each other to jump. On this side, there is Old Eell's barn, where Janie used to store cheap vodka. Next to it was a huge pile of rocks left over from the mining.

The reason I couldn't see it from Janie's house is that it's not there.

"Micah," Dewey says as we pull up. "Listen, don't freak out—"

I am already out of the car.

The Metaphor was enormous and ugly and now it's only missing.

Dewey follows me.

His hands are in his pockets when I turn and stare at him.

"Where is it?" I ask.

He kicks the ground. Technically it is still littered with the stupid rocks, but the mountain is gone. The entire landscape is different. It almost looks nice now.

"What the hell happened? Does Janie know?"

Dewey doesn't look at me. "Of course she knew. She threw a fucking tantrum. Not like that made a difference."

"Why didn't you tell me before? Why didn't you tell me about this first?"

I turn and look around. It shouldn't come as a surprise now, everything disappearing. But it does, my blood is in my head and I don't remember which way is up anymore.

I start forward toward the rough rock-strewn circle, darker than the rest of the shore, where Janie and I spent every Thursday afternoon since fourth grade.

Gravity is irrelevant.

My head hits the ground. Pain is everything, and that is when Janie comes back. Because she knows that I cannot understand living without her.

Her fingers are in my hair, her lips at my ear. "Of course I know that."

I don't open my eyes.

"Of course I know."

But if I were to open them, she'd be there. Her hair like fire falling into my eyes as she leans over me.

"Janie," I say. "Janie."

She smells like cinnamon and vodka. Lemons and sleep.

Someone is dragging me to my feet. Dewey is swearing in my ear, so it can't be Janie. But I keep my eyes closed still.

It's crazy. I'm going crazy.

"You're not *going* crazy," she whispers to me. "You've been here for ages."

Once upon a time

The Journal Of Janie Vivian

Once upon a time there were two beautiful
kingdoms. The prince of the first kingdom
was golden and kind and the pride of the
kingdom. The princess of the second
kingdom was good and lovely and had a
very large ~~trust fund~~ dowry. The fell in love
at first sight and swore to love each other
forever, because of course they would. Of
course. He gave her flowers for her hair and
she gave him gold for his treasury, and they
were horribly, desperately happy. On their
wedding day, both kingdoms rejoiced, and
their day went on far longer than it should
have because not even the sun could bear to
stop smiling at them.

But then the prince took the princess back
to his small kingdom and they became the
king and queen, and slowly things began to
change. The king's kingdom was small and

poor—there were no cocktail balls for the queen to dance at and no other princesses drowning in pearls for her to talk to, and she was lonely. She sat in the castle by herself most days and nights while the king took her money and left without telling her where he was going. The king and queen fought and cried and the nights began to last longer and longer, because not even the sun could bear to look at them.

When they could no longer stand it, they went to the fairies and begged them to make them happy again. The king and queen thought the fairies were good, but really they were just stupid, and they told the king and queen that if they should have a baby, all would be well again.

All except one. One fairy warned the king and queen that the child would be cursed, *but no one listened to her.*

Soon after, a princess was born. The stupid fairies came and cooed over her cradle and the kingdom rejoiced and the sun peeked out again, and the king and queen sat together with smiles pasted on their faces.

Of course it didn't last. One day, the doors burst open and the last fairy flew in, furious. "Fools," she seethed, one long finger stretched toward the king and queen. "How dare you? This child was cursed from her first breath. She will not save your marriage, and you will ruin her. Listen well. On her eighteenth birthday, at sunset, she will blow out her birthday candle and be gone from you forever. And then what will you do?"

The king and queen trembled and clutched their princess so tightly that she wailed. And as she grew, they held on ever tighter. Because they would never let her out of their sight, the princess grew up watching them scream and sob. She counted the days until her eighteenth birthday, and the king and queen held on tighter still, avoiding each other's eyes but thinking the same thing: what will we do then?

before

SEPTEMBER 18

"Are you coming over?" Piper asks as the school empties into the parking lot. "I have Chobani. And if I don't learn an entire chapter of calc tonight, I'm going to fail the class."

"I can't," I say. "It's Thursday! Thursday!" I've saved all of my daily allotment of exclamation marks for this moment. (Jeff Martin told me I was too enthusiastic once and tried to limit my exclamation marks. Eventually I told him to fuck off, but, well . . . you know. Bad habits don't die young.)

It has been a preposterously long day. Ander faked sick to skip the psych test and totally screwed over Phase Six, Step Fourteen: study hall date, and then I went to my senior studio and found out that *three* of my bowls had exploded in the kiln, and I had to lie when Mr. Dempsey asked me if I had let them dry before I loaded them, and then I probably failed my word-of-the-day quiz in Spanish, and then the cafeteria didn't have parfaits at lunch even though they always have parfaits at lunch on Thursdays.

But Thursday is Metaphor Day, Janie and Micah Day, and that's the only reason I didn't fake cramps and go home early. Piper waves and I blow a kiss back, and we go off in our separate directions. I love Piper Blythe and everything about our no-commitment, zero-accountability, convenient-as-hell friendship. No one gets mad when texts aren't answered or plans are blown off, because we both get the big picture. This is high school, and no one really wants to remember high school. In a few months, we'll walk off the stage at graduation and spend the summer together, we'll text each other for the first few weeks of college, and then we'll lose touch. And that's okay. The world is so much bigger than the two of us.

I throw my backpack in the backseat and the sun comes out—same moment, literally, and I throw my head back and arms out and laugh. People are staring and I drink that in too, because I'm Janie Vivian and I'm *alive*.

I open my eyes and I see Micah, immediately, two rows across and halfway down the lot. His grin turns all blushy when I catch him, and he tries to turn away but I grab our soul and tug, hard, and his eyes snap back to mine.

"Race you," I mouth to him, and he's already in his car because twin telepathy, duh.

"Cheater!" I yell as I dive into my car. People are staring, so who cares? Who cares if I'm loud? We are young and free and careless. We are laughing and reckless and *us*.

(Not that they know that. They just think I'm crazy and too liberal with exclamation marks, and they're totally right.)

He's out of the parking lot before me, but I still have the advantage, because my car probably won't fall apart if I drive over fifty. Micah's car proves that miracles are real every time it starts. Also, he's going to slow down at the crosswalk because he doesn't want to run over the middle schoolers. Not that I *want* to, of course, but natural selection was coming for the slower ones, anyway.

(Kidding! Mostly.)

But he does stop at the crosswalk and I floor the gas pedal, and sure, the crossing guard doesn't scream after him, but he's not winning anymore either. I roll down the windows and flash *loser* back at him as I tear through the town, past the tutting grandmothers (one of whom might be mine? I go by too fast. Oops) and the cross country team and the new Moms Who Walk club. My tires set the road on fire and my laughter tickles the sun, and two minutes and thirty-seven seconds later, I'm braking hard and skidding to avoid driving straight into the Metaphor.

I leap out of the car and spin around, ready to do my

touchdown dance in Micah's losing face, but—where is he? Ugh. I knew his car was going to give out. What's the point of a glorious victory if no one's there to witness it?

So I sit down against the Metaphor to wait with all the calc notes I didn't take. I shove a few more rocks in my pockets and lean back, and slowly, the Metaphor starts to swallow me. I tilt my head back and smile at it. "I love you too," I say.

And I do, truly, madly. We found the Metaphor when we were ten. It was early in the summer and we weren't supposed to leave the neighborhood, and we didn't *really*, if you think about it. The signs at the town limits say WEL-COME, NEIGHBOR in a font that looks a little too close to Comic Sans, but if everyone is a neighbor that must mean that all of Waldo is just one neighborhood.

Micah was hesitant and sweet—*ugh*, so many feelings for ten-year-old Micah. He was floppy-haired and shy and freckly and awkward and newly bespectacled and he just wanted to stay in the backyard, and it was my duty as a citizen of the earth to show him how big it was. (And it still is. The earth is awfully big. I'm going to see all of it) We rode our bikes through evil old Ms. Capaldi's lawn and down a few roads and took a few turns and then we were at the quarry like magic.

Everyone warns you about the quarry. So a few (dozen)

people have died and disappeared here—why does that matter? It's beautiful here. Sometimes it's so still that you can feel the earth revolving.

I didn't see that, at first, or feel it. The first thing I saw was the Metaphor, which wasn't the Metaphor yet. (It would be in about a minute. Patience, grasshopper.)

It's big enough to block the quarry, which is enormous. Let's just willfully disregard that just about anything would have blocked out the quarry to my barely four-foot eye level. It really is huge. At least (or almost) two stories tall on good days, probably. It's made up of all of the left-over rock scraps from when the quarry still had granite, so the rocks range from pebble to pet sized, and on that day when we were ten years old and the sun was everywhere and that moment was all that mattered, we stopped our bikes at the bottom and looked up and up and up.

"Janie? What are you—"

I was already climbing, or at least I was trying. The pebbles looked steady from the ground, but they started to crumble as soon as I started climbing, and I was back on the ground within a few seconds, probably, but they were worth it.

"Oh my god," I said, my voice all hushed and awed because there was something holy about the pile of rocks but also because I was still breathless from the fall. "It's like a metaphor for our lives, Micah. Wait—that's perfect! The Metaphor for Our Lives. That's what we'll call it!"

"What?"

We had just learned about metaphors that day, and Micah clearly hadn't been paying attention. I was obsessed. I wrote a whole page of them in my notebook and didn't listen while the teacher explained why they were useful, because some things should just be beautiful and useless.

I ticked them off. "Metaphor one: it's impossible to climb. Inevitably, you end up on the ground with your breath knocked out of you. Metaphor two: see these?" I picked up a rock and held it up to him, but when he reached for it, I retracted my hand. I didn't actually want to let go of it. I put it in my pocket. (Later, I'd write a Virginia Woolf quote on it: *Fear no more.* In case you doubted that this was the beginning of everything.) "See how smooth they are? Smooth and all the same, like thoughts that people kick around until they're smooth and all the same. Metaphor three—"

"They're not all the same," Micah argued, squatting and squinting at the base of the Metaphor. "You're just not looking close enough. Most of them aren't even the same size."

"You're ruining my moment," I said, and we argued back and forth like we still do, and we never did get to the third

Metaphor. But the point is that that was the first time I climbed and fell off the Metaphor, that was the first time I had a rock in my pocket, that was the first time we were really and truly free and alive and us. We were born that day.

I kick my calc stuff aside and get to my feet and start climbing again. I was going to wait for Micah, but I can't stand it any longer. Climbing is always the first and last thing I do here. One of these days, I'll get to the top. I will. But today I'm only a few feet up when I finally hear Micah pull up. His door slams, and I hop back onto even ground before the Metaphor can throw me.

"Late much?" I ask him as he comes toward me. He has a piece of paper crumpled in his fist. I frown. "What is that?"

"This? This is a goddamn speeding ticket," he snaps. "You rushed ahead and almost killed a fourth grader and got the attention of every grandma in Waldo, and now I have to pay a fucking two hundred dollar fine for *speeding.*"

I shrug. "Wouldn't be a problem if you drove faster."

He throws his hands in the air. "That doesn't even make sense! Janie, I'm serious, I have no idea how the fuck I'm going to pay for this and my dad is going to kill me—"

"Oh, don't be a drama queen, Micah," I say, waving the ticket away. "You still have money from Pizza Rancheroo."

"God dammit, Janie, this happens every single fucking time! You get away with shitloads and I'm left with—"

"Shhhhh," I say, throwing back my head. "Micah. Hey, Micah. Look at that."

He looks up without thinking and squints. "What?" He still sounds annoyed. "What am I supposed to be looking at?"

"Nothing. Just the sky. Isn't it beautiful?"

He opens his mouth to snap something else, but he takes a deep breath instead. "Whatever. Can we just do calc already? We're like three weeks into school and I'm already going to fail. Do you get this optimization shit? Because I don't."

Of course I don't. Neither of us is meant for calculus. I can't see the world in numbers or molecules. I just can't. When I look around, I see colors smells motions beginnings. I see sky and wind and hope like birds and art like fire and every desperate wish ever made.

"Oh, forget calc," I say, and dive into my bag for my book of fairy tales and a pair of scissors. "Here, help me make feathers."

He's paging through his notes, frowning and squinting. The sun makes the pages too bright and the wind blows over the Metaphor to ruffle his hair and his annoyance grows on his face like mold.

"Micah, look." I wave my hand in his face. "I'm making wings, remember? I told you."

"Huh," he says, barely glancing over.

I sigh, tragic. "Fine. I'll do it myself. Hey, are you coming to wrestling regionals next week? There's gonna be a fan bus."

We have one of the best wrestling teams in the nation. Maybe because they're good, but probably because we're also one of the only schools where wrestling is a fall sport instead of a winter one. Ander tried to explain to me once why we had to be different, but I wasn't really listening because I was too busy imagining him in a skintight uniform.

"Hell no."

"Why not? I want you to come. It'll be fun. I've never gone to a wrestling match before." I don't really care about wrestling. I'm rooting for the wrestlers because my ten-phase, six-month, totally *non*-creepy plan requires cuddling on the bus back from regionals, hopefully celebratory, but I'll take consolidation cuddling too. Ander's going crazy. It's adorable. I haven't seen him in a while because he's got a scholarship riding on his state ranking, which all depends on regionals. Or something. I don't know. I just know it's important to him and I get to see him in a skintight uniform.

Ander Cameron in a skintight uniform. I sigh and stretch

out, and my foot knocks Micah's notes into the wind.

"*Shit.* God, Janie," he snaps. "I just organized those."

And he's not even a little bit joking. He's not smiling at all, and when I see that, words flash in neon in my head: *how did we get here?*

Micah saved my life once. We were in second grade, and my appendix exploded and the hospital was really ridiculously low on my blood type. (My dad threatened to sue, but my mom didn't want to and it was her money, and they fought about how he was anal retentive and she didn't care enough, blah blah blah.) But Micah and I have the same blood type because of course we do, and the doctor knew because there's only one hospital in Waldo so the doctors know everything. He asked Micah to donate even though he probably still weighed less than a Chihuahua then. Micah thought about it. (Can't you just picture it? Baby Micah with his head of overflowing curls and his brown-green-gray eyes taking over his face, all scared and determined.) He hugged his dad and told him that he wasn't really mad about what had happened with his mom, and he went with the doctor.

Because he thought he was *going to die.*

Later, he came to visit me, all wrapped up in bed, and I grinned at him through the meds and said, "Did you really think you would die by donating blood?"

He muttered something about a movie and blood loss. He said the doctor had had the kind of voice that made everything into an ultimatum and used words that were too big and it had been an honest mistake, and *no*, he wouldn't do it again.

He totally would, though. I knew that.

I guess what bothers me now is that I don't know if he *would* do it again. Sometimes at lunch I watch him and Dewey flicking food at each other and I just can't remember how we got here. We used to know each other to the bone. But now that we're not talking every single day because I live across town in a house I fucking hate and we can barely look at each other in school, I think he's starting to realize how differently we grew up, and in different directions.

Eventually he takes the book of fairy tales. After he reorganizes his notes and opens the textbook to the review pages and writes down the problem numbers and acts like he's actually going to work, like either of us understands optimization and related rates, like that's what we're actually here for. And then he does that thing where he doesn't sigh, but the air comes out of his nose with a little more force than necessary, and he finally takes the book from between us.

"Okay," he says. "So, what? Just ovals?"

"Here, I already made the pattern. It's not that difficult."

He glances at me, and then down again. I don't look at him. I cut a little harder than I have to and snip off the edge of a nail by accident. I chew on the inside of my lip, and Micah sighs, really sighs this time, and his breath makes the feather I'm cutting flutter. He gives in. "Oh, fine. Tell me about the wings."

"Okay," I say, and he laughs because it comes out so quickly. "You know Leo da Vinci's flying machine?"

"The one that didn't work?"

"Yeah, that one," I say. I reach across the fairy tales and start sketching on Micah's calc review. "See," I say. "I'm using wire and bamboo for the main frame, and these"—I draw the wing fingers—"these here are going to be just wire. You remember the pantyhose and wire sculpture I did? Freshman year? With the spray paint? It's going to be like that, but bigger, a hundred times, with feathers instead of spray paint. I think I might call it *Icarus*."

"Why?" he asks. "Icarus's wings didn't work either. And that's not really a fairy tale."

Why is he stomping all over my dreams?

"They did work," I say. Keep calm. "They totally worked. Daedalus made it across the sea fine. You know what Icarus's problem was? He loved the sun too much. He loved fire, like me. He saw the light and he loved it more than anyone. There are things worth dying for."

Micah leans back against the Metaphor and raises his hand to block the sun from his face. "Oh, come on, Janie. What happened to hating clichés and all that?"

"Huh?"

"Dying for love?" He rolls his eyes and shakes his head at the same time, so it just looks like his eyeballs are loose. "You're such a romantic, Janie. Is that part of your whatever-step plan with Ander? Fall in love, die for him to prove your devotion?"

"You're such an asshole, Micah."

I didn't mean to say it. But I don't take it back.

I want to take his condescension and shove it up his nose.

Instead I take a breath. I push the feathers and calculus aside and scoot until I'm sitting in front of him, our legs crossed and knees touching. He doesn't look up, but it takes effort now. He wants to; I want him to too, and our soul is so tired of straining.

"You know Mr. Markus's key to happiness?" I ask him.

Every year, on the last day of classes, Mr. Markus tells the seniors the key to happiness. That's it, really—no one knows anything else, because the seniors have never spilled, ever. No one has ever teased the secret out of Mr. Markus before he was willing to tell it, and the suspense has been driving me crazy since we were freshmen.

Micah snorts. He's a disbeliever. He still won't look at me, either, so that's annoying. He's doing it on purpose.

"I've decided that I'm going to get it early," I tell him. "I don't care what it takes."

"I'm sure you will." It's not a compliment.

I leap to my feet. I give up. I don't want to leave and I don't want him to leave, but right now the friction on our soul is making me itchy. I glare at the Metaphor.

You and me, I think, and begin to climb again.

The stones do the same sliding thing, and there's nothing to hold on to. The whole thing is crumbling as I climb, so I climb faster. I use our soul as an anchor and a rope—friction is useful that way. The Metaphor crumbles, and I climb faster. The rocks fly all over, but I keep going, and—

"Janie? What the hell are you—holy shit."

And that makes it all worth it. I'm not at the top—not yet—but I'm higher than either of us has been before, and I beam down at Micah before I spread my arms and shout, *"Right here."*

"Right here what?" asks Micah.

I drop my arms and blow him a kiss. "Don't you feel it? Just listen. Don't you feel it, Micah? This is where the world is going to end. I'm giving you a front-row seat to the apocalypse. So what do you think? Music, Micah.

Everything needs a good soundtrack. The apocalypse most of all."

He thinks for a long time. That's one of my favorite things about Micah—he always takes these kinds of questions seriously. He always thinks that I deserve an answer. "Rachmaninoff, maybe? 'Prelude in G Minor.'"

"Really?" I say. I can almost touch the sky. I'm stretching so hard that I feel the tension in every cell, every atom. "I would have gone with the Beatles. 'Let It Be.'"

He watches me and I watch the sky, and I smile because it doesn't feel like the world is ending at all.

after

NOVEMBER 24

I've been thinking a lot about being a suspect. Some about how I've never been one before. Some about how it could be true.

Dewey only has to remind me of that a few times before I can remember on my own. I'm starting to remember better, I think. The police help too. I know now that the fatter one is Gibbs. I'm still working on the other one.

They are at school the day I go back. The doctors said my memory probably wouldn't get better anytime soon because they can't figure out why I keep forgetting things. They think it might help if everything just goes back to normal. I guess that's okay, because I'm bored of Metatron.

It's a Monday when I go back. It's raining. I don't remember much else. I probably go to English and calc, and it doesn't matter that I don't remember because I wouldn't have learned anything anyway. The police are here and pulling people out of class for the arson investigation. It's official now. They can only talk to people over eighteen who want to talk back. Dewey tells them I don't want to, but that isn't true. I do want to help, because I can't stop thinking about being a suspect.

Mostly I wonder if Janie is ignoring the police like she is ignoring me. I text her every day and she never responds, and I guess it must be because she doesn't get service in Nepal or something. I wish she would just talk to the police so they know that we didn't do anything. I wish she would just come back and help me remember. I wish she would just come back.

I asked Dewey if she can even refuse to talk to the police when they're investigating arson, if she's even allowed to be out of the country, and he told me to shut up.

He also told me that Ander is a suspect too, because he's Janie's boyfriend and because they traced the gas purchase to his credit card. Wes Bennet swears they had already left the party when the fire started, and Ander says he lost that credit card before wrestling regionals. But nobody knows whether or not they should believe them yet.

I don't remember wrestling regionals, but Dewey tells me we lost.

The less fat detective tells me that it took less than ten minutes for the house to burn.

Gibbs tells me that it started on the second floor. It didn't spread from the bonfire like everyone thought.

He tells me that someone spilled and spilled gasoline there, so much gasoline that there is nothing left of her room at all.

He tells me and watches me for a reaction, as if these things will help me remember.

He also tells me that I'm a good kid, but I figure if I really did start the fire, that won't matter much.

He also asks me what I knew about Ander and Janie.

"Nothing," I tell him. "I knew she liked him. She had this plan to get the two of them together. It worked, huh?"

"Was he ever violent? Specifically with Janie," he asks me.

I blink. "I don't know. Was he?"

Gibbs shifts and looks uncomfortable. "We talked to some of her friends. You know, Carrie Lang, Katie Cross. They said—" He pulls out a notebook and flips through it. "They said that she was upset. Maybe afraid. They think he might have hurt her."

"Oh," I say. "I don't know. I don't remember."

Gibbs sighs and closes the notebook. "Her parents don't know anything, either, so we can't do anything if he did."

He watches me for a reaction. I don't really have one. I just don't remember.

Eventually he sends me back to class.

I don't go back to class. I go to the art room instead. If anyone asks, I'll say that I forgot which class I was supposed to go to. Or that I forgot how to get there.

The art room is in the workshop wing. The senior studios are a series of closets next to it. Down the hall, Dewey is probably smoking in the metals lab with other slackers. Janie skips class all the time here too, but not really. She just bats her eyelashes and tosses her hair and teachers write her passes to wherever she wants.

I go to the art room, but I don't remember how I get there.

Her studio is empty. I've only been here one other time, at the beginning of the year. I stepped inside and filled it; it was tiny and dingy and badly lit and had no windows and she must have loved it, because I had barely been there for five seconds when she started shrieking that I was bumping into things and ruining it all. Back then it was already full to bursting. I remember. Her weird-ass crap spilled off the shelves.

There's only dust here now.

I close the door. The movement stirs the air, and I smell her. The room still smells like cinnamon and vodka. Like lemons and sleep. Like her shampoo and the overpriced tea she ordered from a website that gave her computer viruses. I keep telling her that she's probably drinking bong water, and she keeps ordering it.

It's so empty.

I wonder if she brought it all to Nepal with her.

I wonder if she is happy in Nepal.

I wonder why she will not text me back.

I sit down and the dust puffs up. I cough. My eyes water. I blink and blink. Maybe I blink for a few seconds or maybe I blink for hours, but when I stop, I see rocks in the corner. Rocks from the Metaphor, and they are in my hand though I don't quite remember reaching for them. I have to blink a few more times. It's very confusing. I keep thinking that I've finally gotten used to it and then I forget again and it's confusing again.

I turn the rocks over and over in my hands and think about how she only left rocks in places she'd probably never see again.

I sit there with the rocks in my hands until the lunch bell rigns.

It rings and keeps ringing. I put the rocks in my pocket and go to the cafeteria. I don't remember getting there, either. I guess it doesn't matter much. The hallways are ugly anyway.

The cafeteria is loud and full of people. It is too full of people, because I run straight into someone else.

Janie always says that my main problem is that I don't know how to walk away from things. I think she's wrong. Walking away isn't the hard part. Turning around is.

I should have turned around.

I should have turned and kept my head down before Ander Cameron could see that it was me.

"You," he said.

Me.

"What the hell did you do, you little shit?" he demands. "You two, the two of you. What the hell did you do? The police won't fucking leave me alone because of you."

What did I do?

What did we do?

Hell, what didn't we do?

For a moment, it's funny. I smile by accident.

Ander Cameron takes another step toward me and swings his fist at my face. It connects with my jaw. My tray goes flying and so do I.

In researching for my stupid senior project on apocalypses, the only thing I really found interesting was all of the different ways people think the world is going to end. I read Wikipedia pages and collected catastrophes. An enormous snake is going to swallow the world. Fire and brimstone is going to fall from the sky. Freezing. Flooding. Four horsemen and a whore. Falling stars and empty oceans.

It doesn't end like that, though.

What it actually feels like when the world explodes, the instant it explodes, is nothing.

The explosion doesn't hurt at all. It doesn't hurt until you hit the ground.

Again.

My head cracks on the linoleum and my tray lands on my face and the soup is in my nose. Somewhere above me Ander Cameron is telling the unlucky bastard on lunch duty that I slipped, and perhaps for the first time in his life, no one backs him up. The monitor drags him away, but I am still on the floor.

I understand why Janie did the things she did. I understand why she wanted everyone to like her.

It sure as hell beats this.

There are people all around me, and it's hard to focus on most of them. I think Dewey must be there, because someone has been swearing for the last five minutes. I look around, and around, and I see Piper. She hangs back with fingers pressed to white lips.

Janie would never have done that. She would never stand

back and watch. Janie would have been brimming with wrath. For her friends, she would have done anything. Anything. She didn't kick or punch. She flayed, slowly, with eyes too bright.

Sorry, I tell her. *Sorry you made such shitty friends.*

Something moves above me and I figure it's someone else telling me to get up, but it's not. It's Janie.

"God," she says. She sits on one of the tables and grips the edge, legs swinging. She looks at me. "So many assholes. Asshole here and an asshole there. Old Waldo had a farm and called it high school."

She jumps off the table and lands beside me. Her head is cocked to the side and her hair is spilling across her collarbones. I wait for her to reach out a hand and pull me up. She doesn't.

What she does is lie down beside me, so that we're both on the floor in the spilled soup. Her fingertips reach out to brush mine, and I pull away because my hands are still covered in clay dust. She would freak if she knew I'd been in her studio.

We just lie there.

Neither of us helps the other up.

Eventually the lunch monitor does get me up. She sends me to the nurse, who tells me to call my dad to take me home, or maybe to the hospital in case my stitches have split again. I pretend to talk to him, and go to the lobby to wait.

I wait until no one is watching me and then I walk out the door, and keep walking.

It has stopped raining.

I walk through the park, which takes me a street over from my house. But I keep walking. The quarry is only 0.72 miles from our houses. Her old house and my house. Really, the new one was just down the street.

It starts raining again. It's okay. We've always liked water. No, that's not right. Janie loved fire. She loved markers and rocks and fire. I like water, though. I like the way it waits, and when you touch it, it both moves away and clings to your finger. I like the way it rises, like memory, or fear. You told me once that I was made of water, I think. I don't remember. I don't remember again but

what if

it just

doesn't

matter?

My head hurts.

My head hurts a lot and the world is spinning because of it. By the time I get to the quarry, it has turned upside down twice.

I have to sit down or I'll puke on the Metaphor, except—
oh, of course. It isn't there anymore.

Some things are easier to forget than other things, I'm
noticing.

I sit at the edge of the quarry and look over the water.
The loose rocks left behind from the Metaphor that is gone
dig into my ass. The water seeps into my shoes.

The water climbs higher, or I slide lower.

Oh, look. A memory.

Her hair in my lap. My feet in the water, which is cold but
not unbearably. The sun is burning our skin. A book of
fairy tales is open on her stomach while she scrolls through
her phone, which keeps vibrating. The wind is turning the
pages back and forth.

"Does the Metaphor look smaller to you?" she asks me.

She is squinting up. Her hand shades her eyes. "Maybe it
just looks smaller. Do you think it could be sliding lower?"
she asks. "Or the water's climbing higher?"

"It doesn't look different to me," I say. I am too lazy to turn
around to look. My fingers were in her hair. I always liked
touching her hair, because sometimes it was hard to believe
she was real. Her hair was soft and smelled like lemons.

"There are only four weeks and two days until our
birthday," she announces. "Did you know that? I have a

countdown. Can you believe how warm it is? I love the sun, Micah. I love it as much as it loves me. Are you listening? Stop looking at my phone."

I catch the words *Nepal* and *volunteer trip* before she closes the tab.

"Four weeks and two days, Micah," she says. "We're going to be *adults*. We're going to drink tea with our pinkies up and do whatever the hell we want because that's what adults do. That's all I want for my birthday this year. Ha ha, just kidding."

I touch her hair. The strands both move away and cling to my finger.

"What do you want, then?"

"I want a bottle of wine so big that the cork can plug up the hole in the ozone layer," she says. "I want a poem, or a poet. I want the world with a bow on top. What about you?"

You.

I don't say that, but I think it. I think it with everything I am.

"I think the Metaphor is getting smaller," she says again, and that's all I remember, except her eyes, which are only blue because they reflect the sky, or the water.

The water.

The water climbs higher, or I slide lower.

The water is cold, and the rain is turning to snow. The sky is falling down. The sky is falling faster.

"Janie," I try. Her name is stuck in my throat blocking my breath.

My breath comes too fast and too shallow.

The water climbs higher, or I slide lower.

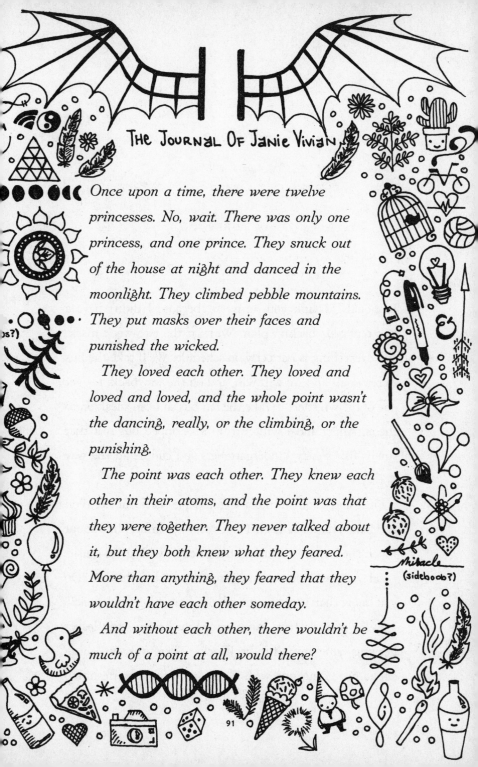

THE JOURNAL OF JANIE VIVIAN

Once upon a time, there were twelve princesses. No, wait. There was only one princess, and one prince. They snuck out of the house at night and danced in the moonlight. They climbed pebble mountains. They put masks over their faces and punished the wicked.

They loved each other. They loved and loved and loved, and the whole point wasn't the dancing, really, or the climbing, or the punishing.

The point was each other. They knew each other in their atoms, and the point was that they were together. They never talked about it, but they both knew what they feared. More than anything, they feared that they wouldn't have each other someday.

And without each other, there wouldn't be much of a point at all, would there?

miracle
(sideboob?)

before

Regionals! Thank you, universe, because I didn't have a non-regionals backup plan. We're at the two-week mark, and everything is perfectly on schedule. We'll take the bus to regionals and we will win, and on the way back, I'll get one of the wrestlers to take the fan bus so I can sneak on to theirs. Ander and I will curl up in a ripped bus seat that smells like snotty kindergarteners and cuddle all the way home.

Piper and I squish into a seat and she takes out her iPod and hands me an earbud. There's another thing I like about Piper: she has great music. I trust people with great music.

"Hey, Pipes!" someone calls from the back of the bus. "Do you know that Wes has one of your bras in his backpack?"

A lot of girls hate Piper, probably because she leaves her bras lying around in backpacks. There was something about her going out with a senior during our freshman year, and then she cheated on him with another senior, and by the end of the year she'd had sex with half the senior class, which wasn't true. Piper's hymen is more intact than mine is, probably. But Piper is very pretty and she's also very aware of it, and people just don't seem to like her very much.

But I like her.

And people like me.

The boys start using her bra as a slingshot, and I think about telling them that bras are freaking expensive, but Piper just keeps playing a game on her phone, and I figure that if she doesn't care, I don't need to worry, either. Under Piper's amazing playlist, the game plinks away.

"Hey, Pipes," I say a few miles later. "How's Wes?"

"Stupid," she says. "Like usual. We went camping last week, though. Having sex in a tent? Not fun."

Okay, so maybe not quite as intact as mine.

She sighs and takes out her earbud and twists it around her finger. "And then he told me that he just wants to be friends with benefits. Who even says that? 'Friends with benefits'? He can't just say 'hook up' like a normal person? He's a tool. And now my mom wants to get me on the pill, but her gyno is such a freak, you know? And she doesn't want me to go anywhere else."

I didn't, really, because my parents would never have let me go camping with *Micah*, let alone Ander.

"Not fun?" I asked. "Not at all?"

"Well, more fun than this is going to be."

I elbow her, harder than I probably need to. "Stop stomping on my dreams," I say. "This is going to be fabulous. Ander in a skintight uniform all over another hot guy? Um, *yes*."

She puts the earbud back in. "Just wait."

Oh.

Okay, I see.

Wrestling is really gross. And . . . a little terrifying? All I can really see is a tangle of arms and butting heads, and Piper is laughing at my expression as I lean back as far as I can. The sweat is *flying*. My body is practically between the legs of the guy behind me, but he doesn't really seem to mind.

Ander is on top, on the bottom, on the ground, on his knees, back on his feet, slammed on the ground again, clawing back up. Ander is *strong*, muscles, clenched arms flashing in a way that I thought would be hot but actually makes me wonder if I want to cuddle with him at all, if it's totally completely one hundred percent safe. He's brutal, hands around sweat-slicked shoulders, arms around neck— *is he supposed to do that?* Do people die at these things? Are there ever any audience casualties?

"Oh my god oh my god *ohmygod*," I say, as the other guy rams his shoulder into Ander's chest and they go flying, literally flying, and hit the floor so hard I feel it in the risers. Piper looks bored.

"I told you," she said. "I said we should go to Starbucks, but nope."

The ref does the whole floor-slapping thing and then everyone (not us) is cheering, so I guess that means it's over. I catch sight of Ander's face when he finally peels it off the ground, and I know it's over.

He's not going to state. He's not getting his scholarship.

He stumbles toward the risers like he barely remembers he has feet. He rips off his helmet and his blond angel hair is plastered tight to his scalp. I'm moving before I know why, running down the rickety stairs and calling his name.

He stumbles right into my arms, and he clutches the back of my (favorite, now sweaty) dress and his hot, hot tears bleed through the fabric and right into my heart. He smells rancid, but I hug him tight around his perfectly narrow hips and tell him that it'll be all right, all right, all right. All right?

"All right," he answers. All right.

And then he kisses me.

I am drowning in saltwater, burning tears and hotter sweat, and the crowd—which had been so terribly quiet after he lost, all three fan buses of people gone dead silent—erupts, *howls*.

We are the center of the universe.

Then he breaks off and rests his head on my shoulder for a moment before he pulls his soaked shirt over his head and walks off to the locker room. I am wet where his saturated skin brushed me, but I don't care. My fingers are still on my lips, my lips on fire, and the crowd is still cheering for us, and Piper laughs from the sidelines and squirts me with a water bottle. I watch Ander go and imagine him in charcoal: bone and muscle and salt and sweat. I memorize him walking away, head bent and shoulders curved and vulnerability radiating like angel wings.

"I love you, Ander Cameron," I whisper, trying them on my tongue.

They taste like ice. They melt in my mouth and disappear. Stomach butterflies and air.

I thought they would taste more like peppers and chocolate and pop rocks, like putting a Mento in your mouth and washing it down with Diet Coke. I thought it would be bubbles and breath and heat and spinning.

But they're words, little moments, and they pass.

That's okay. That's what moments do. And I want to remember moments, bright and perfect, because you're allowed to do that. You're allowed to Photoshop. You're allowed to crop things like the way Ander held me too tightly, how he held my wrists instead of my hands, how it never occurred to him that I didn't want our first kiss to be like that.

Besides, kissing a sweaty Ander in front of a crowd trumps phase ten ice cream kisses on the swing set anyway, right?

I'm pushing myself toward yes when I see Dewey in the stands, and I do a double take when I see Micah with him. Oh, right, I told him he should come. I didn't really think he would. His eyes are on mine and they're wide, wide, wide.

Oh, god.

He mutters something to Dewey and then he's coming down the bleachers, and I'm all frowny and awkward trying to figure out what to say to him. What? Yes, I know that Micah is in love with me. Of course I know. I will be in love with him someday too. That's obvious. We're predestined. But can't that wait? Can't I just kiss my sweaty scary angel boy in the meantime?

Oh. He wasn't even coming for me. He's leaving the gym.

I look around to make sure no one's watching, and then I follow. "Micah," I call, and I finally catch him a few hallways down, grabbing on to his shirttail and pulling him to a stop. He doesn't turn around.

"I can't believe you actually came," I say to his back.

He shrugs. "Dewey wanted to. Same reason you did, probably. Find some stupid wrestler to hook up with."

I swell. "I'm not *hooking up* with Ander. I have a plan! We're perfect."

He laughs. It's not a nice laugh. "Not the word I'd use."

"Yeah? What word would you use? Awkward? Oh, wait. That's you."

Too far? Too far.

"Oh, I don't know." He totally does. "How about shitty, like everyone you've ever gone out with? Conceited? Shallow?"

My mouth falls open. "Are you fucking kidding me? Are you really going to pull that shit? You want to talk about shallow, Micah? Why are you here with Dewey? It's not like you actually like him. It's not like you two are even decent people to each other most of the time. You came with Dewey because you know he's in love with you, and you need that, don't you? You're so desperate to feel wanted that—"

My throat closes. I blink, rapidly, but what's the point? Micah probably felt my tears before I did.

He walks away, and I let him go.

after

DECEMBER 2

It was Dewey that found me. He came over to use my Xbox and I wasn't there. I guess he took me to the hospital, where they said things like nervous breakdown on top of selective retrograde amnesia. They ask me over and over again what I was doing, and I don't know. I don't, I don't know.

Dad took me out of school and put me in therapy. I was supposed to go to therapy anyway, but I told him I could manage. I didn't need to. We couldn't afford it. We still can't, really, but Dad is insistent, which he rarely is.

I don't know how many times I tell him that I wasn't trying to kill myself. I don't know what I was doing. It doesn't matter. I went to piss yesterday and caught my dad counting my pills.

I don't get it. Why me?

Why the fuck is this happening to me?

It's Tuesday, so we're going to therapy again. Whatever is playing on the radio is shit, but I don't change it. My dad drives with his shoulders up to his ears, but he doesn't change it either. I guess it's better than driving in silence. We don't really remember how to talk to each other.

"How's the online school going?" he tries at one point.

"Shitty," I say. "Not that that's any different than ever."

On the first day, Dewey skipped school with me. We ordered pizza and played Metatron for fifteen hours straight. I woke up with a piece of pizza on my chest and a penis drawn on my upper lip. I picked up my controller again and died another sixty-seven times. I started jumping off bridges around level seventeen. There were too many bridges.

Dad gives a strained laugh. "That bad, huh?"

I shrug, and count the trees as they go by.

I get to ten, but that can't be right.

"You started over a few times," my dad says.

I guess I must have.

Dad walks me into the building and past the receptionist and hands me over to Dr. Taser, whose name is actually Taaser and pronounced something like "tosser." I pretend not to remember when she tries to remind me.

"Micah!" she says as I walk in. She looks like antiseptic

and smells like too much perfume. My dad stands in the doorway and they talk in low voices about me, and I sit on the couch.

"He's struggling today," I hear my dad say. "It's been a hard week."

They notice me watching. My dad leaves, and Dr. Taser closes the door.

"Do you need anything, Micah?" she asks. Her teeth are too white. "Water? Coffee?"

"I'm fine," I say.

"All right, then," she says. She's still smiling. I don't think I've ever seen her without a smile. "So tell me about—"

"My week was fine," I say. I count the ceiling tiles while I talk. Twenty down, thirteen across. I think. "I like my new online classes. Yes, I think it helps me relax to not be in public education eight hours a day. Yes, I know that my dad wants to be there for me more but can't. Yes, I know you think Dewey is a great friend. Yes, I know where I am. Yes, I know I will be okay."

She flounders. That was supposed to take the entire hour. This is my third session, but she's predictable as hell. How do you feel today? How do you feel right now? How do you fucking feel?

She clears her throat and taps something into her iPad. "I'm glad to hear that, Micah. Do you think you might want to talk more about Janie today?"

Janie? Janie is sprawled on the couch, pushing me into the armrest. Her head is in my lap and her hair spills everywhere. I am careful not to touch it. Her eyes are almost colorless and they bore into mine.

"No," I say.

"Maybe we can start with something easy? A happy memory. You must have so many of those."

"So many," Janie echoes. Her hand traces slow circles on my kneecap. "Us. You and me, Micah. You and me."

I swallow. "Stop," I whisper. "Stop."

I know she isn't here. I know she isn't real.

And yet her fingertip on my knee, shifting and feather light, is the only thing that keeps me grounded.

"A happy memory, Micah," Dr. Taser prompts.

"The old mental hospital," Janie whispers. She sits up and places her lips by my ear. Her breath is warm in my hair. "Veet in Carson Eber's shampoo. Condom balloons in Stephen Mackelry's locker. Counting rocks at the Metaphor. Come on, Micah. You can choose anything."

Rocks at the Metaphor.

Janie counting the rocks at the Metaphor because she was sure they were disappearing. Counting, counting. Ten, over and over again. Rows of ten.

I remember the rest.

~

Four weeks and two days before our birthday. It was
September 10. We went on a Wednesday that week—I
don't remember why. Her parents kept texting her to go
home, and she couldn't wait until she was eighteen and
didn't have to listen. Four weeks and two days.

"I think the Metaphor is getting smaller," she said, and
sat up. Her hair brushed my wrist. "I'm sure, Micah. We
have to count the rocks. And again next week. And if
there's less next week, we'll know."

She walked to the Metaphor and sat at its base. She
looked up and her face looked like prayer for a moment
before she began to count.

"One," she said, putting one aside. "The number of balls
Hitler had."

"Ball," I corrected. "And I don't think that's actually
true."

"It doesn't matter if it's true," she said. "People believe it.
That's all that matters. Two. The number of times you've
actually let me drive you somewhere. I can't believe you're
walking back. Just let me drive you."

"Um, no," I said. "I'm not getting into your car."

"Why? I have candy!"

"I don't want to die, that's why. Janie, you were supposed
to be driving slow and you still almost killed a fourth

grader just now. I'm not getting in your car."

"Whatever," she said. "Your loss. Are you going to help me count or what?"

I kind of just wanted to lie there, but then she threw a pebble at my forehead and said, "Count!" So I rubbed my forehead and sat up, and picked up a rock.

"Three," I said. "Um. Uh. Three. The number of, um, wishes in a lamp?"

"God, Micah, you're so lame," she said.

"Yeah, I know," I said.

She started to reach for a rock, but she stopped when I said that. Her head tilted to the left, just a bit. She stared at me for a long moment, and then she sucked half of her lip into her mouth and chewed on it before she said, "You're not really, you know."

"Jeez, Janie, I was just kidding—"

"You're not lame. You're—you're, just, like, a decent human being, you know?"

"Wow," I say. "High praise right there."

"No, I mean . . ." She huffed out a breath. "Like most people aren't, you know? Not really. They just pretend when they're at school and in public, but they're not actually good. They just want people to think they are. But you—you just are. You actually are."

I scratched my head so she couldn't see that I was

blushing. "Okay, so are you going to count the rocks or what?"

And the moment passed. But I kept thinking about it.

She threw another rock at me. "Six. The number of pieces of pizza I ate the first time we ordered here," she said.

"You skipped four and five."

"I threw two at you." She threw another one. It bounced off the rim of my glasses. "There. Now you have to start at eight."

"Okay," I said. "Eight. The number of pieces I ate before I threw up."

"Oh, god, don't talk about it. Don't don't don't."

"Nine," I said, "the number of seagulls that showed up to eat it."

"Micah, stop. *I'm* going to throw up."

She stopped asking me to help after that. She put them in rows of ten, squares of a hundred. She got to six hundred before she gave up. We stretched out and she fell asleep and her hair smelled of lemons and the sun burned us bright, and I thought about what she said. That I was a good person. That she was not.

"Micah? Micah, just breathe for me, okay? It's all right."

Fingers on my knee, circling. Hands on my back, patting. Here, now. I take a deep breath and blink. Dr. Taser stands over me, and she is no longer smiling.

"Sorry," I say. "I'm sorry. I'm fine. I know where I am. I'm in your office, and I'm fine."

Janie traces letters on my knee.

LIAR

The Journal Of Janie Vivian

Once upon a time, there was a princess, and she had a plan. She was going to a ball. She planned for weeks and weeks—she made a dress and borrowed a carriage and found a back door that no one looked after. Sometimes things went wrong, but there were always miracles, trees that gave her golden dresses and fairy godmothers who gave her glass shoes.

On the night of the ball, the princess sneaked out of the house and went to the castle, where there were beautiful ladies and stacks of cakes and lots and lots of vodka. There was also a prince made of angel parts and perfect, perfect teeth.

The prince took her hand and they danced the night away. Everyone cheered for them.

There was only one part of her plan that could not be fixed by fairy godmothers or

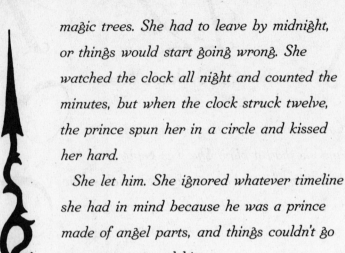

magic trees. She had to leave by midnight,
or things would start going wrong. She
watched the clock all night and counted the
minutes, but when the clock struck twelve,
the prince spun her in a circle and kissed
her hard.

She let him. She ignored whatever timeline
she had in mind because he was a prince
made of angel parts, and things couldn't go
too wrong around him.

Right?

before

OCTOBER 8

Ander and I are a whirlwind. Of glitter and puppies and everything that's good and right in the world. We are perfect and beautiful and I've already gone through two tubes of Chapstick. It's like every day I date him is the best day of my life.

Today is off to a great start too. Over breakfast, my parents told me that Dad got called to an emergency meeting in Utah and Mom's going with him because their marriage counselor says that their Janie-less time is a vital pillar of their marriage. They're going away again in a few weeks because it's really, really vital. *Gag.* They're very, truly, horribly, terribly endlessly sorry to leave me alone on my eighteenth birthday, but they'll bring me back wonderful presents and lots of them, so I assured them that I'd be okay. I came to school and Piper brought me coffee and I invited her and Ander and a bunch of his friends over to help me celebrate my adulthood.

Ander kissed me when I told him, or maybe I kissed him. Who cares? Literally everyone because they were all watching because the two of us are too damn perfect.

It's like I can really get to know him now, really *see* him. I look at him and I see freshman year, when he had just gained a foot in a summer and it seemed like it was still giving him vertigo. I look and I can just see his second-grade class picture—the crooked teeth and the haircut he did himself the night before, and the eyes the color of maple syrup.

And I see me too, Freshman Me with her new back-pack and schedule clutched in sweaty fingers, looking around corners to find classes and—*"Ohmygod here comes Ander Cameron."* I wasn't even friends with Piper then, was I? No, so it would have been someone else's shoul-der that I turned and buried my face in. Who was it? It doesn't matter. I used to look at Ander and imagine waking up with him. Stretch, yawn, see him beside me, smile. I wanted to talk to him and be friends with him and try out a different kind of living with him—the kind that happened with your lips.

Sometimes, back then, I'd see him and he'd see me, and he would blush and I would blush and our mutual blushing was like—like how Disney told me that love at first sight would feel.

And sure, he became more of a douche.

And sure, I became—

I don't even know. I became *me*, less so and more so.

And now that we are Officially Going Out, it's everything I thought it would be. It's so damn easy. Zero percent commitment, a hundred percent fun. He's started wearing his thick Ralph Lauren sweaters again—you know the ones, the big chunky-knit things made of boyfriend material—even though it's not quite sweater weather yet, and every time I see him, I bury my face in his chest and thank God that fall is a season.

And best of all, he pretends with me. He pretends that we're crazy in love, pretends that the air is our love and we're swimming in it, and it's just *easy*. There's so much kissing.

Kissing him is so. Much. Fun.

This is it. This is true freaking love.

Until the moment passes.

I get a *now*. I deserve a now, don't I? I do.

And here's what's happening now: AP Bio lab, which doesn't ruin the best day of my life because it involves fire. I don't read the lab closely enough to figure out why, and Piper is being an amazing friend by doing the experiment while I sit on the counter and swing my legs and light matches and blow them out in Ander's direction like kisses. He's across the room and laughing and winking his angel eyes.

(Micah's in this class too, but we're very good about not looking at each other.)

I don't even notice the fire until Piper screams that our lab sheet is burning.

Someone pulls the fire alarm before Mr. Kaplick can tell us to chill, and we're rushing into the hallway and out the door into the sun that keeps the day just above chilly, and I can't stop laughing as the rest of the school pours out. I'm about to lie down and start making grass angels when someone catches my hand.

Ander spins me around with his finger on his lips. I pull it away and kiss him, hard, and he pulls me away and we sprint for the parking lot.

We go to the diner down the road and lounge in greasy seats talking about nothing in particular for hours. He plays with my hair and I order every milkshake on the menu so we can taste them all. His favorite is Clementine Dreaming and mine is NuTELLA Like It Is.

After, he drives me home, and I tell him to stop where the road forks between my new house that I fucking hate and the quarry.

He listens, because that's what boyfriends do. He turns off the car and smiles his crooked smile and leans over and we start making out. I melt like girlfriends do, wrapping my arms around his neck and kissing him back. We love each other with the kind of love that begins and ends with our lips.

Outside the car, the lamplight is fighting the rain. The Metaphor is just down the hill, and I imagine it while he kisses me, the perfect scene: the two of us dancing under shy streetlights, spinning closer to the water, hand in hand, climbing my mountain of rocks and falling flat on our perfect asses. Can't you just see it? I can.

Maybe we even make it to the top together.

I always knew I'd make it to the top one day. I had painted the moment of triumph in watercolor, in oil, in acrylic; I had sculpted it in clay and stone and plaster, welded it in copper and iron; I had dreamed it in color and sepia, oversaturated and in black-and-white. And never once had Ander been there with me.

It was always Micah. Always, anything, everything.

We kiss for a while, until Ander starts getting frisky and I pull away. He never stops grinning at me, not even when he drives me up the hill to my new house, where all the lights are on because my parents have probably been waiting for me to come home for hours now. My lips are swollen and I use the last bit of my third tube of Chapstick. He kisses me again before I get out of the car, and he gives me his jacket to run to the house so I don't get wet.

At the front door, I turn back to blow him a kiss goodbye, but he's already gone.

after

DECEMBER 5

Dewey is in my house again.

Why is Dewey always in my house?

"Dude," he says. "You gotta get out of bed. You smell like ass. You haven't even been getting up to shit, have you. Goddamn, Micah. I brought Metatron: Sands of Time. It's zombie Confederates this time. Come on, get up."

"No," I say.

"Yeah, you know what? We need to get you out of this house. We need to get you some air or something."

"There's air here," I say. I take a breath to prove it. *Look at me, breathing. Look at me, breathing. I'm not a vegetable.*

"Vegetables still breathe," says Dewey.

"Did I say that out loud?"

"Yes, you goddamn said that out loud. Jesus, Micah."

"Oh," I say.

"Jesus," he says again, and glares at the ceiling like Jesus is right there. "Come on, Micah. We're gonna do something. What do you want to do?"

"I want to lie here," I say.

"We could go to the diner," he says, like he didn't hear me. I don't know. Maybe he didn't. Maybe I didn't say it out loud that time. I try to remember, but I already forgot. "Or we could drive somewhere, run over some kids like Janie liked to do, crazy bitch—WHAT THE FUCK, MAN?"

I throw an apple at his head, hard. It's rotten; it splats.

"Oh, fuck it, Micah," Dewey howls, "they were right about you. Goddamn, *goddamn*, you actual fucking *ass*, what the hell? Fuck. You're going goddamn crazy, man. You're one seriously fucked-up little son of a bitch, and— screw you, Micah. God, my *fucking face*."

But he still doesn't leave.

"Get the fuck out of bed," he says, seething, looking around for a clean shirt to wipe his face on. He snatches one up, finally. I think about telling him it's not clean, but I guess he'll figure it out. "You know what? We are going out tonight. I'm going to throw your sorry ass over a cliff."

"I don't want to get out of bed," I say. Yes, out loud, I hear the words out loud. "I want to stay here and feel sorry for myself and imagine the apocalypse."

Apocalypses. Apocalypses are safe.

"Let me tell you about the apocalypse," Dewey says. He strides to the bed and throws my covers back. I shiver and he gags. "Jesus. *Jesus.* You know what, Micah? You're not going to live to see the fucking apocalypse. You're going to get your filthy ass out of bed and we are going to go see this shitshow of a world, or I'm going to murder you right here and you'll never see anything again. Got it?"

I sigh into the pillow, and he's right. It does smell like shit. "Will you just leave? Please?"

"Yeah, dude. And you're going to come with me. Let's go."

So I get up. I go.

The Metaphor is Janie's territory. Dewey and I always do our drinking on the far side of the quarry, where people drown. That's where we go now. There's a ledge where stoners smoke and assholes dare each other to jump. We are both tonight. Dewey has weed and cigarettes and Canadian whiskey, and I keep daring him to jump.

He just lights another cigarette. He cups his hands around the tip and shivers. "Dammit, Micah, will you sit the fuck down? You're making me nervous."

I sit. He hands me the bottle of whiskey. I drink until I almost puke.

"God," I say, coughing. Some of the whiskey comes back

up and sprays the grass, which is already frosty. "Isn't Canadian whiskey supposed to be the good stuff?"

"This is the good stuff," he says. "Just wait until we have to start into the shit wine. You know what you need? A cigarette. Shit offsets shit."

I ignore him and take another swig. And another. Dewey watches me. I watch the other side of the quarry, where someone is running. "Is that Piper?"

"Hell if I know."

"She's always crying," I say. "Every time I see her she's crying."

Dewey snorts. "And how often do you see her?"

Not very. But in school, when I was still in school. Sometimes, she runs by my house and she's always crying.

Another swig. After a while, he tries to take the bottle back, but I lean out of reach and take another swig.

"Seriously, Micah," he says. "How are you doing?"

"I'm cold," I say.

"Micah—"

"I'm fine. My attitude is as bright as my future."

"Micah, stop fucking around—"

"I'm not," I say. "I'm telling the truth."

The truth, the truth. I'm a terrible liar. I take another drink. Dewey stares at me for a while, and then he starts talking about shit I don't care about. He blows clouds around our heads and I drink until I forget.

Drink to forget.

Janie's lips in my ear. "Take another shot."

". . . town is going to shit. I love it. You hear about Ander?"

Her breath soft against my cheek her lips in my ear her body warm against mine.

"Are you listening to me? Suey Park and a bunch of other people told the police that they saw Wes and Ander leaving Janie's before the fire started, so I guess that idiot really didn't set the fire. Shame, right?"

Her breath soft against my cheek her lips in my ear her body warm against mine her eyes colorless and glittering.

"I mean—shit. Don't listen to me. Don't worry about it, man. No one really thinks you did it. They just think that she—that you might have known . . . you know what? Never mind—Micah, what the hell are you doing?"

Her breath my cheek her lips my ear her body against mine her eyes

her eyes glittering and colorless

and the only part of her face I can see

as she tells me to take another drink.

"Micah, Jesus, get away from there."

The only part of her face I can see because she is backlit by the bonfire that rises higher and higher as she tips my cup back

whispering, "Just drink. Forget this. It's okay. I promise, just drink, just forget."

"She told me to forget," I say, spitting the words so that they are real and outside my head. Spitting, as if the momentum will push the memory out. "We were on a lawn chair and under a blanket and the cup was electric blue and she made me drink and drink and told me to forget."

"Micah."

Lips breath warmth.

The whiskey is horrible in my mouth pleasant in my chest fire in my stomach. I take another swig, a long one, and then I say, "I think we did something. Janie and I."

"Micah," says Janie.

"We did something horrible."

"Micah," Janie says again. Her voice is burning. "Don't."

"What? She told you to do something and you scampered off to do it like her little bitch? Yeah, I'm not surprised."

"She doesn't want me to tell you."

"The two of you were so fucked up," he says, but he isn't taunting anymore. He takes a long drag on his cigarette and the tip burns the color of her hair. His voice is low and tight.

"She says that you can't ever know."

Dewey blinks, and then he's squinting at me. "What?"

"Micah, stop talking. Stop talking now."

"She wants me to stop talking," I say.

"Micah. Micah, hey. Look at me." He taps the side of my cheek. The cigarette is too close to my ear. I think I can see it burning out of the corner of my eye, but that could just be Janie. It could be her hair. "Micah, man. You're saying she's here? Now?"

"Yeah," I say. "She says that she hates you."

My legs are over the side of the ledge now. The water is far, far below, probably. The quarry is two hundred and nineteen feet deep. It is the deepest quarry in Iowa. It's dark. I can't see. I don't remember when I got this close to the edge.

Dewey's face is so white that it glows in the dark. "Dude, do you want me to—do I need to take you to the hospital or something?"

"Nah," I say, and take another swig. "Damn, Dewey. Isn't Canadian whiskey supposed to be the good stuff?"

The bottle is empty. The bottle goes flying. Dewey smacks it out of my hand and it goes flying. Distantly, there is a splash as it falls into the water.

I squint into the dark. "There's like a five-hundred-dollar fine for littering."

"Screw the fine." He's in my face. "There's been, what,

fifteen people who've died here in the last fifty years? If they can't find their bodies, you think you're going to find that stupid bottle? Look, Micah, listen to me—"

"Fourteen," I say. "The last one was Patty Keghel in 1972. I remember. I was looking up local apocalypses and came across her name because she was a big Herbert Armstrong follower. She believed every one of his false apocalypse predictions and once she ran naked through Waldo to alert everyone. She used to fish in the quarry and she made her own rafts, but I guess not good ones because that's how she drowned."

Dewey goes quiet, so I keep talking.

"Janie and I saw her grave. Freshman year, we saw her grave. It's in the cemetery. Do you want to see? We should go see. We can go now."

"What the hell are you on right now—"

"And again," I say, spitting again, "again this year, we came here. Here."

"Yeah, I know we've come here before. We get drunk here all the time because we're the biggest shits on the planet."

"Not you and me. Us. Janie and me. Me and Janie. I remember that. I remember now, it was our birthday. We came and there was a boat. You made a treasure hunt and it led to you."

"Micah. What the fuck are you even saying? Are you talking to her?"

"Yeah," I say, and I turn to Dewey but a little too fast, and his hand is on my arm and I am leaning on him because I can't feel my feet. "She won't—she won't leave me alone."

"Oh, stop exaggerating, Micah," Janie says. "You don't want me to leave you alone."

"She's my soul mate," I say, and I say it again, but I can't make it clearer. The words are mashed in my head, vomit in my mouth. "My soul mate. Or not soul mate. She said that we shared a soul. What does that mean? She said that we were an atom. I don't know, Dewey. I think she's crazy."

"I am crazy," Janie says. "So are you. All of the best people are. Who said that?"

"Lewis Carroll. Lewis Carroll said that."

Dewey is holding his cigarette so tightly that it's disintegrating in his fingers. Maybe he's imagining that it's me. Squeezing all of the insanity away. "Micah, seriously—"

"She's goddamn insane, man. But I love her, Dewey. God, I don't know how to stop loving her. Sometimes it fucking hurt to look at her, you know? You ever love someone like that? No, you haven't."

"You don't know that," Dewey says. All of a sudden, his voice is so sharp. He cuts through the haze, and it hurts, hurts everywhere.

"It hurts," I say, and it's almost a sob, it sounds like a sob. Am I crying? I don't know. I don't know. "It hurts, Dewey, it hurts so fucking bad. It feels like I'm dying, Dewey, like my head is fucking tearing itself apart. I just want her to come back. I just want to know why she didn't ask me to go with her, I just need her to text me back—"

I'm on my feet and the ledge is higher than I thought and I'm staring down and down and it's too dark because there's no moon tonight just like there was no moon that night and I can't see anything but the height. I look to the side and Janie is looking up at me and everything is blurry and she is the only clear thing in the world.

And then I'm falling and falling and falling

but

in

the

wrong

direction.

The Journal Of Janie Vivian

Once upon a time, there was a boy in a tower. His hair never grew long enough so that he could climb out, so for a long time, he just watched. He watched and watched until he knew the angle of the moonrise and where the stars crossed and how the geese flew. He watched anything, everything.

Which was nice and all, but someone had to show him that there was more to life than watching. Someone had to drag him out.

That's where the girl comes in. The girl was the best kind of crazy. She got her luck from matches and threw rocks at his window and coaxed him out, one word at a time. She did it because she wanted to, because she needed to, but also because she didn't want to be alone. It wasn't fair to keep that kind of boy locked away.

But life's not fair. So there's that.

MORE. THAN. ANYTHING.

before

OCTOBER 9

Yes, *fine*, I still feel guilty. What? I do have a heart. A big, messy, bleeding-like-a-volcano heart. If you pulled it out of my chest, it would be covered in escaped butterflies and black holes and weeds that look like flowers.

It has been six days since I've talked to Micah. That has to be some kind of record.

And tomorrow is our *birthday*.

Sure, Ander fills me full of butterflies that get all tangled in my heartstrings, but Micah adds gravity to all of my black holes. He waters my weeds.

He hasn't even *looked* at me since regionals. And he has such nice eyes.

Insert grumble here. Oh, all right. They could almost even be called bedroom eyes. Maybe.

So, I don't know. Maybe it's guilt or maybe it's just that I want him to talk to me again or maybe it's *our freaking birthday tomorrow*, but I skip school today, after my parents climb into their cab to the airport arguing about who was in charge of printing out the boarding passes, to set up a treasure hunt for him. I write a note in ink with a pen that has a real nib (which is totally not the one that Mr. Markus is still looking for), and I stain it with coffee and burn the edges and everything. I sneak into his house through the door on his deck and leave it on his bed, along with an ancient Walkman with a CD inside and earbuds wrapped around, and a note that says *BRING ME*. I swipe his binoculars from inside his desk too, because I couldn't find mine, and settle in his bushes to wait.

And wait.

And wait and wait and freaking wait.

Oh, hurry up, Micah. I'm chilly. There's a whole pile of burned matches next to me and still no luck. It's the eve of our *birthday*. Don't do this to me. But it seems like he just might. It's getting late. I'm about to sneak back into his house and grab the note before he can see it and spare myself some horrible humiliation and also maybe give up on the kind of friendship that keeps the whole freaking world turning—

Yes! There he is! Ninja to mission control: subject is driving onto premises. He pulls into the garage and I raise my (his) binoculars. A minute later, the light in the kitchen comes on, and then the lights in his room. I tiptoe out of the bushes so I can creep on him better. I'm getting a cramp in my neck and I can't stop thinking about how much easier this was when I was across from his window, but at least I can see him rubbing his eyes before he flops out of sight onto the bed—NOOOO! My note! Oh, come on, Micah, it's barely ten. You can't go to bed yet. Roll over. Damn it, I spent so long on that note! Get up. Get up—oh, okay, I guess that works. He rolls onto his side, and the note—oh, my poor baby—must crinkle or something, because he sits up, confused, and feels around for it. *Finally.*

He reads it, and then he crosses the room and opens the window. I'm almost too slow diving into the bushes. He looks around and just stands there for so long that I'm already deflating, because of course this wasn't enough, of course he's still annoyed, and he and I will never talk or look at each other again just because of that one stupid fight at regionals, and our soul will wither and crumble—

His shoes! He's looking for his shoes! His lights are out! He's going back to his car!

And now I'm rushing too, and I can't stop grinning. My half of the soul is dancing, my half is light, and I dive into myself and tell it to shut up, because Micah's half is totally going to feel it, and the surprise will be ruined. Nope nope

nope. I won't allow it. I spent too much effort on this. On us.

Keep quiet.

Tiptoe through the freaking tulips, soul.

Micah starts up his car, which probably starts an earthquake in Australia. I count to sixty, and then I run after him.

I run three blocks over to where I'm parked. The world is wide, and the moon is rising.

I put my hand in my pocket before I start the car and squeeze. *Fear no more*—I don't even need the reminder, or even the Skarpies or matches. Tonight, tonight, there is nothing I have to black out. There is nothing I have to set on fire.

The note had read, "Once upon a time, there was a boy and a girl who found a tree and fell in love with it, until the witch cut it down."

Micah's car is nowhere in sight, so I don't even know if he's going in the right direction. I think he knows, I think he remembers. He has to. I turn down the street, freeze, and throw the car into reverse. Oh, thank god. He did remember. And he didn't look back.

Ninja mode activated. And maybe just one more match.

I park my car behind some willow trees and send a silent sorry to Ms. Capaldi's lawn. I mean, she's pretty old. Maybe she won't see the tire tracks.

Before we got the guts to leave the neighborhood, before we found the Metaphor and the rest of the world, we used to come here all the time. It must have been second or third grade. We came every day, because Ms. Capaldi had this fantastic tree in her backyard—a real tree, not the wimpy toothpicks you see on everyone else's lawns. The trunk was so wide that when Micah and I hugged it on opposite sides, we couldn't get our hands to meet. The lower branches were too heavy to grow upward anymore, and there were places where gravity took them back, and they rooted there and grew again. I never climbed, really, but Micah did. No, he scurried. He pulled himself higher, higher, and I stayed on the ground and kicked the trunk because my climbing skills were pathetic.

I used to think this was the most beautiful place in the world. I used to think that this was the place where the world began. But then in third grade, we came after school and the tree was in pieces, hacked and ripped and ruined, and I burst into tears. Ms. Capaldi explained that the tree was dying, but I didn't care. It was freaking tragic. Micah had to drag me away, and I cried all the way home.

So Ms. Capaldi ruined my childhood and I just ruined her backyard. I call it even.

Now there's a stump, and when I peek around the side of

the house, Micah is sitting on it with the next clue in his lap. Is he smiling? It's too dark to tell. I think so. I hope so.

It's a flashlight and a calendar page from the September of our freshman year and a bottle of peach vodka.

He's too far away, but I feel him relax. I feel his laugh, even if I don't see it—I feel the air shift, but only between the two of us. He clicks the flashlight on and casts it around, and I slam myself against the side of the house and suck in my breath. The light passes and I put my fingers behind my back. No shadow puppets tonight.

The light clicks off. Then on. Off on, on, pause.

Morse code? *Code!* I *knew* making him learn it would come in handy one day!

You're the world's biggest idiot, Janie Vivian.

And I'm grinning like it.

I hear his engine a bit later, and I tiptoe back to my car and follow. There are three texts from my dad telling me that he and Mom have checked into their hotel and to call them when I can. Improvement! Usually, there would be a few phone calls and a voicemail or seven. There's hope for him after all. I send him a quick "I will later!" and drive to St. John's Cemetery.

Which is actually, as far as cemeteries go, really pretty. Not overly groomed. Overly groomed cemeteries are so *wrong.* Cemeteries shouldn't have lawn-mower tracks. They should have wildflowers and dandelions and wishes and tears. And tonight, under the angel with the wide, wide wings for a certain Michael van Pearsen, 1920–1977, I HAVE LOVED THE STARS TOO FONDLY TO BE FEARFUL OF THE NIGHT, there is also a clue.

(It was only the most perfect epitaph ever. I Googled it later—it was by Sarah Williams, and I am *sosososo* jealous because I didn't die quickly enough to claim it first.)

We first came here two nights before the start of freshman year. I slid my bookshelf across the space between our houses and climbed into Micah's room with a slim bottle of peach vodka that I'd (over)paid Beaver Rossily from across the street to get for me, and we walked 1.58 miles to the cemetery and got drunk for the first time.

I hadn't wanted my first time getting drunk to be, I don't know, *sweaty*. I didn't want it to be at a party with people I didn't know. I actually wanted champagne, but Beaver said I didn't have enough money. It was fine, though. The peach vodka had *burned*, but we choked it down and laughed fire out of our noses.

I remember that the stars were huge. Enormous. They were worlds, and that night, ours was as bright as any of them.

I remember that it was endlessly funny that we were in a cemetery. I remember that we lay down under the angel and laid our hands over our stomachs like we were dead, but then Micah slid his hand into the space between our bodies and I took it, and it was warm and sticky with vodka. I remember threading my fingers through his and pressing our life lines together.

I remember planning our funerals. I wanted blue flowers, all kinds. Forget-me-nots and cornflowers and bellflowers, irises and pansies and hibiscus. I wanted them anywhere, everywhere, in my hair and on my coffin and on the tables at the reception afterward.

I had asked him if funerals had receptions.

No, Micah told me, weddings do.

Then I want blue flowers at my wedding too.

What else?

I want rain, I told him. I want thunder and sobbing. I want cursed wifi so people who use it will grow nose hair so long they trip over it. I want a hot minister and a church full of people and chocolate, honey cookies, and cinnamon candles and handkerchiefs the color of the sky.

For the wedding or the funeral?

"Both," I said. I want it all, I want everything.

Micah had wanted the normal stuff. A coffin, a hole in the ground. But he wanted a yellow tie. I remember that specifically, because I remember picturing it: a tie made of sunshine.

I wonder what Micah remembers. I wonder if he remembers the same things, or if he remembers the other parts. There must have been other parts. We must have walked back—what had that been like? Stumbling and laughing all the way back under streetlights. I should ask him later. We'll lie on X-marks-the-spot and piece together the memories.

That had been a good night.

Tonight will be a good night too.

I don't even get out of the car. The next one is a fast clue, just a bunch of sparklers. Besides, Micah is all jittery around cemeteries now. I don't think he'll stay long, and he doesn't. I see him half jogging out of the cemetery and jumping into his car. I take a breath that pulls all the air in my car into my lungs, and then I roll down the windows and follow him.

Down the road, to the school, and farther. To the forest on the far side of the quarry that was supposed to be cut down and made into a nice neighborhood full of picket fences, but they ran out of money almost as soon as they started. So now it's just this cluster of trees that desperately wants to grow into dark fairy woods, and once in junior year, Micah and I went there with a bunch of sparklers. No reason, really. It was finals week and we needed something beautiful. We sent them high, and the embers rained down and burned our bare shoulders.

By the road to the quarry, Micah goes straight and I make a left. He'll go to the forest and find a pair of paddles sticking out of the ground and a rock from the Metaphor balanced on top, and he'll know where to go. I have to beat him there.

It's dark now, aggressively dark, and I open my window and stick my head out to make sure there are stars. It's freezing and I'm prepared to be annoyed, to huff and puff at the sky and blow the clouds away, but no, there they are! Baby stars blinking and waking and stretching. Don't be shy, baby stars! You can shine. You can even fall, if you want. Just not tonight. Tonight is mine.

I take a deep breath. I feel the darkness in my lungs and it feels right. I start toward Old Eell's barn, filled to the brim with the night. The barn is farther down the shore than the Metaphor, and it's unfamiliar territory in the dark, and unfamiliar is terrifying, so I pee before I go.

What? Fear makes my bladder wonky.

Old Eells is the ghost who lives in the barn and drowns the faint of heart, and I know he's not real because Alex Brandley always brings girls here on first dates and he should have drowned a thousand times over by now. He brought me here sophomore year and tried to go through three bases in a minute, and I told him I'd kick him in the balls but they were too small to find.

But he did show me the boat, so I guess it was worth it. I've taken over the barn now. Micah and I have a stash of alcohol behind the rusty tractor, and it makes me feel terribly grown up. I ignore that tonight, since Micah is bringing the special peach vodka I left for him. I go to the back corner instead, where the boat is. It's not heavy, but it's still heavier than I'd like it to be. I kick it and lug it and then something rustles over by the tractor and it's probably a starved wolf so I *run*, hauling the boat behind me, until I'm at the edge of the quarry. I leap into the boat and wrap my arms around my legs and squeeze my eyes closed. No spiders no rats no snakes no bats no wolves. Nope nope nope.

"Janie?"

I scream.

Micah yelps too, and he drops everything he's holding, and I'm out of the boat and his flashlight is in my face and I'm screaming again, screaming, "Did you break the vodka? Is the bottle broken?"

"Jesus Christ the vodka is fine I am having a fucking heart attack!" he yells back, and then we're in the grass and laughing, and everything is okay, okay, okay.

"You took forever," I tell him when I can breathe again.

"Yeah, I wandered around that goddamn forest for a

while. You couldn't have done this, like, during the day?"

Well, we could have, if you were home. But I don't say that. I say, "But it was more fun in the dark," and he shakes his head and smiles and says, "I guess."

"Well, we're not done. Come on. Last clue," I say impatiently, trying to tug both of us back into the boat. But Micah digs his feet in.

"Wait," he says. "That's the boat from the barn."

"Get in the boat, Micah."

"I'm not getting into the boat. No. No way."

I consider stomping my foot. Overload? Overload. I glare at him instead. "Why not?"

"Oh, I don't know," he says. "I don't really want to drown tonight."

"You're not going to drown," I say impatiently. "I keep telling you, it's totally safe. Alex Brandley takes girls out in this boat all the time. We'll be fine. You're like, half his size. If it doesn't sink while Alex has sex in it, it won't sink with us in it."

"Oh, great," he says. "Unstable and ridden with STDs."

But he pushes the boat into the water and climbs in, and then I run and leap into it, and the boat wobbles and we cling to each other, but it doesn't tip over, and we don't drown. We are nervous laughter and fast breath and faster heartbeats, alive alive alive.

And then we calm and become a different kind of alive, the kind that requires music, so we take out the Walkman and push earbuds into our ears.

"Indie shit," Micah complains, but he hums along. And the next track is Liszt, and his fingers tap against my palm. Eventually we are on our backs, hands pressed together.

We are Janie and Micah, Micah and Janie.

"Let's play a game," I whisper. I am the quiet and the quiet is me. "Let's play Secrets."

"Okay," he says, like I knew he would, like he always does. "You start."

"I peed in the quarry before you got here."

He quickly retracts the hand he had been trailing in the water. "God, Janie."

"What? I had to pee. Before I got in the boat. Or else I would have peed in the boat, and—"

"Okay, okay," he says. "Um. Uh . . . I still do the lightning bug thing. Like, you know. Put them in jars with grass and stuff."

"That doesn't count," I say. "I already knew you did that. I've seen them on your dresser."

"It does count," he says, sounding annoyed. He's not, really. Just embarrassed, which he shouldn't be. I think it's adorable, and mostly I was just mad that I didn't think of it first. "It just has to be something you've never *told* anyone before."

"Fine," I say. "I ordered a pair of Hunter boots even though I swore I'd never get a pair."

"Yeah, I'd probably care more if I knew what Hunter boots are. I stuck a cockroach in Dewey's sandwich at lunch yesterday."

"Ew ew *ew*," I say, and the boat rocks as I try to wriggle the word off. *Cockroach*. "Ugh, where did you even find one?"

"What, the cockroach? I just—"

"Stop saying that word. I hate that word."

"—grabbed one out of the empty locker next to mine. There's always five or six in there. Cockroach cockroach cockroach."

I try to push him out of the boat. He tries to pull me in with him. We splash each other and we both end up soaked.

"I tried to pierce my own belly button."

"You used that last time," he says. "You always try to use that one."

"Yeah, because I tried to pierce it *again*."

"Yesterday I told my dad that I couldn't believe he grabbed his one opportunity to have an affair, while Mom had so many more and never did."

It's quiet now, just the wind and us. The rest of the world has stopped existing. This is it: the quarry and the boat and the curving sky, and our confessions to each other. Our soul is bare, and we are spilling everything.

Well, not everything.

But he's holding stuff back too.

"I flushed my mom's Tiffany earring down the toilet," I say. "Then I went online. It cost five thousand dollars."

"Did you really?"

"Well, I only flushed one, so I guess it was only twenty-five hundred. So now she just wears the one and leaves her hair down over the other one."

"I told Dewey that we couldn't hang out tonight because my dad's taking me out to dinner."

"My parents think I'm at Piper's because they didn't want me to be alone in the house that they should never have bought, and I'm glad I'm not."

That's not a secret, but Micah just braids his fingers tighter with mine, matching up our life lines. I scoot closer. I push my shoulder against his, and my thigh against his thigh, and I hook my foot around his calf because he's gotten too tall for our feet to match up. And that's how we lie, telling secret after secret as we drift, until I look around and decide that *this is it*, this is the center of the quarry.

"This isn't the center," Micah says when I tell him.

"Why not?" I ask, and he doesn't have a good answer.

I open the vodka. We pass it back and forth, throwing it back and coughing all the way down. We flick water at each other as we wait for it to kick in, and when it does—when the dark is fuzzy and the stars are much closer, I bring out my matches. Micah hands me the sparklers. I aim at the stars and set the sparklers off, and we lie back and laugh at how high they go.

"We should do this again," he says. I watch the fireworks in his glasses.

"Nope. No repeats. Just live the moment, Micah."

He doesn't argue. "Something else, then," he says, and his voice is cautious, almost shy, and I lean back against him. I put my face in his shoulder and breathe him in, memorize the way we fit together.

"Something else," I say. "After tomorrow. Then we can do anything. Anything."

"Right. You can legally have sex with Ander," he says, and his voice gets further away with every letter of every word.

"Micah," I say, closing my eyes. "Don't. Not tonight. Hey, what time is it? Can you check? My phone is dead."

He squints at his watch. "Twelve fifteen. Almost."

"Happy birthday, Micah Carter," I say. "This is my

present, by the way. I hope you like it." I put my face in his side and smile. "We're eighteen, mostly."

He pushes me away, and for a second I wonder if this isn't enough, if he's still angry, before I open my eyes and see him shifting so he can pull an envelope out of his pocket.

"What's that?" I ask, already reaching.

"Happy birthday, Janie Vivian," he says, shy.

I open it and begin to cry.

"Oh my god," I whisper. "Oh my god, oh my god, oh my god, Micah. What did you do? Did you really?"

They're tickets, and brochures, and phone numbers and emails and a map to Nepal.

"This is the trip." I still can't get my voice louder than a whisper. "Oh my god, oh my god, oh my god, Micah. Did you really? You can't do this, it's too much—I mean, I'm going to take it, obviously. But Micah. *Micah.* I can't believe you. How did you know?"

He laughs. "Are you kidding? You've been looking at that page for months and closing it if you thought anyone was looking. You even didn't start your college applications, did you."

It's not a question because he already knows the answer. I can't stop sniveling. His smile is everything.

"You have to pay me back," he says, but he still can't stop smiling for long enough for either of us to take him seriously. "I only got it because I knew you'd never go unless someone told you it's a good idea."

"Oh, shut up, Micah," I say. I love him more than anything. I grab him and drag him against me, full-on sobbing into his bony shoulder. The boat wobbles and Micah shouts a warning and his head bumps mine and we collide. We are whole again, we are us.

"So there," he says, "now you know what you're doing next year. Good Samaritan Janie Vivian. I still have no idea where I'm going to be—"

I slap my hand over his mouth, because I'm not done admiring my tickets, and none of that matters right now anyway. Tonight. This moment is all that matters.

"We have this," I tell him, and drop my hand from his soft, soft lips. "This is ours."

"This," he says, and the word is so quiet that it seems to stretch on forever.

Later, as we paddle back, I ask him, "Did you get it? The treasure hunt?"

"Um, I guess. Was it your way of saying you're sorry you were a total bi—"

"It was the elements," I say. I tick them off on my fingers, starting with the middle one. "First was the tree, and climbing, and into the sky, the air. And then the cemetery, for earth. And the fire, and the water. And the last one."

"Ununoctium?"

"Us," I say. "You and me. We're the last element, you idiot. I love you more than anything."

"I love you more than everything."

Janie and Micah. Micah and Janie.

after

Dewey is reaching for me and he is missing, his voice in my ear. He spits *fuck shit goddamn* at me, and the moment splits: us, here now, and also not us, not here.

Dewey's fist is slamming into my jaw, his voice in my ear telling me to never fucking talk to him again.

His eyes are all pupil and the fire is burning higher in them.

I am falling but also already on the ground, and the smoke is thick and my glasses are shattering and Dewey is on top of me. His spit is flying and splattering on my face.

"You asshole." He says it like he means it. "You asshole, you little fucking asshole. You piece of shit, you actual fucking piece of shit—"

And me on the ground. I look up at him through smoke, so much goddamn smoke, and seeing my blood on his knuckles, his hair in his eyes, blue eyes eclipsed by his pupils.

A memory within a memory: *I shouldn't have said that.*

I should have kept my fucking mouth shut.

And then—pain, searing but dull. Focused but everywhere.

Here, now, my head hits the ground.

The impact shakes the memories loose, and they come back in floods.

Helium on her breath. Her voice rising higher as I wondered if it was okay that it turned me on.

Janie climbing the Metaphor. Arms spread wide as I squint and try to find where her hair ends and the trees begin.

The sky and fireworks. The secrets and elements.

She climbs into my bed. We huddle under the covers. The air is humid with her sobbing.

Wings. I remember the wings, I remember them burning. A fire, a different one.

Janie pulling on my sweatshirt and transfering her rocks, her markers, her matches into its pockets.

They come, they fall, faster and faster.

Anything, everything: they're almost equal, but not quite.

I have always needed her more than she needs me.

~

"Goddamn," Dewey gasps in my ear. We're on the ground and the night is dark and I'm cold, I'm freezing. "Goddamn it, Micah, goddamn, we're getting out of here."

He drags me to my feet, and I sway.

"She declared an apocalypse here," I tell him.

"Good for her. Can we go?"

"Right. Go. Barn. We have vodka in the barn. We're out of champagne, though. We drank it all that night. Didn't mean to."

I am swaying from the memories. Dewey hitting me Janie sobbing fire burning. Drink, drink to forget.

"No, not the barn, we're fucking going home—"

But I'm stumbling toward the barn already, Old Eell's where there are ghosts. Ghosts. Janie's ghost? Maybe.

Maybe we drank here too much. We had a stash in the winter to keep warm. And in the summer, to stay hot. That's what she said, anyway.

"Micah, will you just hold on—"

I push the barn doors open and almost fall over. I see the blurry shape of the boat and remember the treasure hunt, remember how easy that was. How she was waiting. How I always expected her to be waiting. Needed her to be waiting.

"Micah, please—"

"Back here," I say, stumbling in the dark to the rusty tractor. It's dark; I lose my balance and then my footing. It doesn't hurt. Something is poking into my elbow. Dewey stops next to me and uses his phone screen to shed a bit of light on us and I see

I see

Matches and Skarpies and rocks. Rocks, but only a few.

"What the hell is this?" Dewey asks. He crouches down and starts sifting through the papers, squinting. "What the fuck? Hey, Micah, look. Plane tickets."

"What?"

He opens a brochure. "Cool. Look at this. You want to go to Nepal?"

He understands faster than I do. He snaps it closed and shoves it out of sight, and glances at me with his mouth tight. I sway on my feet.

Tickets to Nepal.

Janie is in Nepal.

But

but if the plane tickets are here

then

she's not.

And if she's not in Nepal, then

then

I scramble for the rocks. I yell for Dewey to turn on his

fucking flashlight app, and the light is sudden and burning but when the stinging stops and I blink the water away, I see it.

Black against the other ones, smeared by her fingers.

Fear no more.

I can't claim to know Janie Vivian. I don't know if our souls are connected. But I do know this: she would never go anywhere without this rock in her pocket.

"Micah." Dewey's voice finally reaches me, frantic. "Micah, man, can you hear me? Oh, shit. Oh, goddamn, shit goddamn—okay, it's fine. I'm taking you home."

I reach up and clutch his collar, and try to say his name. My lips are slow. "Fuck," I say. "Oh god. Wait. Dewey, wait. I remember. I think I remember."

He doesn't listen, or he doesn't understand. I can feel his body heat and his breath. No one has been this close to me since Janie, that night.

Janie in my arms, hot breath and fingers clutching, lips on mine.

"Oh, Micah." Her voice is everywhere, that night, tonight, every night. *Forget. Forget.* "Forget everything. Burn it all."

"*Shit*, you weigh a ton. Okay. Fuck you, fuck this. Fuck this. Stay here."

I don't know how long it takes me to realize that I'm alone.

before

OCTOBER 10

"No, we always play Never Have I Ever," I whine. My head is in Ander's lap and they're all here on the floor in the basement of the house I fucking hate but that's finally good for something, Piper and Wes and Jasper (who they all call Big Jizz because he spilled milk on his lap in, like, middle school) and Gonzalo and Jude. Happy happy happy birthday to me. "I'm out of Never Have I Evers."

Ander's hands are wrist deep in my hair, and his fingers play with it like it's water. "What, then?"

"Oh, I don't know," I say. "Something fun."

"Never Have I Ever," Piper insists, and we all ignore her.

"We could play beer pong again," says Big Jizz.

"We're not playing beer pong again," I say, and my tongue feels fuzzy. I am spectacularly bad at beer pong. "Oh, Flubber! Let's play Flubber! Wes, get the cards."

"What the hell kind of a game is called Flubber?" asks Gonzalo.

"FUBAR," Ander explains. "Janie doesn't like that, so she calls it Flubber."

"Flubber is such a cute word," I say, and giggle, and can't stop giggling. Flubber, flubber.

"It's a good thing you're pretty," Wes says, coming back with another bottle of vodka and the deck of cards, which he rains down on my face. He drops down by Piper and takes a swig of Keystone Light, and I roll out of Ander's lap and pull the cards across the carpet to me as he explains: one shot for an ace, two for two. Pick three people to drink for three. Answer a question for four. Five for five. Six, everyone drinks. Seven, a round of Never Have I Ever. Eight, everyone drinks. Nine, rhyme, loser drinks. Ten, everyone drinks. Jack, guys drink; queen, girls drink. And king, what do we do for king?

"Waterfall," I say. Trip, stumble, bubble, burp. "Dealer drinks and then the next person drinks and the next person drinks and you drink until you can't drink anymore. Like chicken but more fun."

"It's a stupid game," Jude says, but he takes the deck from me to deal. "All right, let's go. Jizz and I gotta head out after this. My parents are getting back from Des Moines tonight."

"Why does Jizz have to go?" I ask.

"I'm his ride, remember? You're such a lightweight, Janie," says Jude, and throws a card at my face.

"Am not," I say. "You guys are cheaters. You never drink when I get the ball in your cup. At least I'm not Gonzalo."

"Yeah, Gonz." Ander laughs, leaning over to slap Gonzalo's shoulder. "Dude, he's out. Damn, he had like, what, seven shots?"

"Piece of shit," Wes snorts. "I brought the hard lemonade for the asshole and he gets wasted on the good stuff. Typical. Jude, fucking deal."

"Shove it," Jude says, but he flips a card at him. Ace. Wes throws back the last shot of the old bottle and flicks the tiny bit of leftover vodka at Piper, who's sprawled on the ground in a crop top that barely covers her bra. I try to remember what Dad said about the carpets when we first moved, but I only remember that they were expensive. It doesn't matter anymore. We've spilled enough that it doesn't even pay to worry. I'm in one of Ander's shirts because I spilled beer on mine. It has his name across the back in big red letters: C A M E R O N.

Piper flips him off and Wes grins at her, a big blurry grin. Jude hands her a card. Seven.

"Ugh," Piper says. "Okay, okay. Um. Never have I ever . . . never have I ever finished a large order of fries from McDonald's."

"Bullshit," says Wes. "Bull. Shit. Seriously? Girls, man." All fingers down. Mine too. One large order of fries? Please. I've had five. Micah and I went through a phase where we'd go to McDonald's every Metaphor Day. We built Jenga towers out of fries and threw them at ducks.

"There you go, Janie," Wes says appreciatively as my finger goes down. He snaps my bra strap and snaps it again, picking me like a guitar. "At least you know how to live."

How to live. I am living, living, living.

Jude hands me a three. "Me," I say, "Ander, Piper."

We throw our heads back and the vodka rushes down my throat and drowns all of the butterflies. If it didn't taste like burning, it might have tasted like apples. Apple vodka, one of my dad's fancy bottles. Micah once told me that he thought that he hated vodka. I don't hate vodka. Vodka is easy. I don't even need a chaser for vodka, not for vodka.

They cheer me on.

Ander gets a ten. We all drink. Jizzy gets another seven. We all drink again. Jude pulls a nine. "Nine," he says.

"Wine," says Wes.

"Swine," says Piper.

"Line," says Ander.

"Vine," says me.

Sign, dine, mine, incline, aine. "Aine?"

We all look at Ander, who's very, very blurry.

"What?" he says. "It's a word. Old English or some shit. It was in the Shakespeare we read in class. Right?"

"No, shithead," says Wes. "This is America. We play American FUBAR. Drink."

He drinks.

And we go and go and go. Queen, five, ace. Ace, three, nine.

"This game is too complicated," Jizzy complains, probably because he only has two brain cells: one that's in charge of making sure his hair is perfect every morning and one that's a balloon in his head, pushing on the sides of his skull so he thinks he's smart. He grabs a bottle of vodka for the road and kicks Jude. "We should go."

"Yeah, sure," says Jude, and he leaves the deck while Wes calls them faggots.

"I don't like that word," I tell him. I try to frown. *Come on, caterpillar eyebrows. Work with me.*

"I don't like you," he says, and it's true. Wes told Ander when we first started going out that he'd rather jump into the quarry than date me.

I don't mind him. Wes is the kind of person that isn't worth the effort of disliking.

"We're going," says Jude. He tries to pick up Gonzalo, who wakes up long enough to shout "No homo!" and stumble out. I wave at them, and it's exquisitely funny that Gonzy can't walk. He misses the door and hits a wall.

"Well, fuck them," says Wes, and throws a two at Piper, who bats it away like her hand is heavier than gravity.

"I'm tired," she mumbles, and curls up like a kitten. I pet her and laugh and laugh and laugh.

"Jesus, Janie, shut the hell up," says Wes, and digs through the deck until he finds a ten. "Dude, you start," he tells Ander, and Ander throws back the rest of his can.

I go. Wes goes. Piper raises her head long enough to lap at her cup.

Ander. Me. Wes. Piper. Ander. Me. Wes. Piper.

Ander.

Me.

Wes.

Piper.

Until the world is swimming in us and we're swimming in the world.

"Ugh, I'm done," says Piper, curling back up.

Ander, me, Wes. Ander, me, Wes. Eye contact and middle fingers, until Ander lunges forward and knocks Wes's shot glass out of his hand and all over Piper. Piper squeals and her voice echoes in my brain. Wes tells Ander to fuck himself, but "Whatever," he says, "I was done anyway, I'm not fucking insane."

And then it's just Ander and me. The whole world is just Ander Cameron and Janie Vivian. Ander and Janie. Janie and Ander.

Wait, that's not right.

But I want to win.

Except the glass is spilling and spilling and spilling, and suddenly it's not in my hand anymore, and I try to catch it but Ander is cheating, somehow, and I can't move, I can't move right.

Wes shouts "Champion!" and slumps onto Piper, who rolls her eyes and starts getting to her feet, pulling Wes with her, heading for the door. I try to watch them go, but just then Ander's syrup eyes wrap around my wrists, "Sorry Janie I guess I'm just better sorry I'll make it up to you."

And then he's kissing me, his hands in my hair and his lips on my lips and his breath hot and wet and too loud.

"No," I say, but it gets lost on the way out of my mouth and Ander swallows what's left of it. He kisses me again and again, and his hand—where's his other hand? His other hand is in my shirt, his shirt, and crawling crawling crawling up.

Far, far away, Piper says they're leaving, and I don't, *I don't want her to leave.*

Wait, wait, wait for me, Piper. "Piper, no, stay. Stay."

I see her look back, her eyes my eyes and the moment is still, but—

But she turns.

She pulls Wes after her and they go up the stairs and they're gone.

And suddenly I'm freezing, frozen, and Ander is drawing slow circles like he's trying to warm me up with his ice fingers.

"Ander, Ander, stop. *No.*"

"It's fine," he says. He's in my ear, kissing and licking, and then his hand is too high in my shirt and I try to tell him, I tell him I'm tired, I'm so tired.

"Okay," he says softly, his breath is in my mouth, his arms are behind my head and knees, big strong wrestler arms, and the world is spinning. I blink and we're on the stairs, and then he's pushing the door to my room open and I'm on the bed. It's okay, I think, it's okay okay okay—

—but then—

It isn't, it's not at all, because Ander is there too,

and me not knowing, not knowing, but knowing *now*, knowing that I don't want to, I don't, I don't. He's on my bed over me and he's kissing, kissing, kissing. Touching, touching, touching.

"Ander," I say. "No. Stop."

"I have a condom," he says, and kisses me again before I can say no again.

"Wait," I say, and he says, "Don't worry, they're gone, it's just us, it's just you and me."

Not you and me, *never* you and me, not Janie and Ander or Ander or Janie. Where's Piper? Piper has to come back soon, she will, she will. I want to be Janie, alone, just Janie—

But then he's pulling at my shirt, and I try to keep it on but he says it's his shirt, it's his. I try to get to my rocks, my Metaphor rock, *Fear no more,* but it isn't there, it's *his.* And the bra, the pretty pretty bra that gave me cleavage, real cleavage, is gone. And then the panties, matching and matchingly gone, and the world—

—it freezes, it stops turning and we are forever and infinitely trapped in this moment, this moment of Ander and Janie together and I fucking hate it, I fucking hate it, *I fucking hate it.*

"Just relax," he tells me.

And I close my eyes and think, *Maybe it won't matter.* Maybe I'll wake up tomorrow and I won't even remember this. Maybe it will never have happened.

The Journal Of Janie Vivian

Once upon a time, a princess took a few shots of apple vodka. She took a few more and fell asleep. A prince kissed her awake, but all she really wanted to do was sleep.

She told him that, but he didn't stop.

She did tell him. She told him no *and* stop, *but did he listen?*

Did anyone, ever?

PART II
Happily Ever After

after

DECEMBER 6

Forgetting is the easy part. This should be unsurprising, but it surprises me. Forgetting was easy. Remembering is endless and it hurts, endlessly.

On the night of the bonfire, on the last night that anyone saw Janie Vivian, it was too cold to be outside. I was in bed with my laptop on my chest when Janie came up the stairs. She had been gone all day. She was gone most days, actually. I see less of her now that she's living in the basement than I did when she was at the new house.

She stood in the doorway, and I knew something was wrong.

Her eyes were almost colorless. Her hands were deep in her pockets and her pockets were full of stones. I could see them, knuckles and rocks.

"What's wrong?" I asked her. "Where have you been?"

She leaned her head against the doorframe. "What are you doing?"

"Senior thesis," I said. "Have you heard of Thomas Müntzer? He said the world was going to end in 1525. Listen to this: he dies under torture and gets his head cut off, so I guess it was pretty damn apocalyptic for him."

"Shouldn't you be getting ready for homecoming?"

I shrug. "I've got time."

"Micah," she said. "I'm sorry."

I blinked up from my screen. Her hair was falling into her eyes and she didn't move it away. "What?"

She sighed. "Don't be that guy, Micah. I said I was sorry, okay?"

"I know, I just mean—" She always said that guilt lived in my side of the soul. Janie never had anything to apologize for. People forgave her without being asked. I squinted at her. "Is that my sweatshirt?"

She looked down. "Yeah, I guess. They don't make sweatshirts like this for girls, you know?"

"Uh, not really," I said. I pushed my laptop aside and started to get up. She crossed her arms and curled over a little. She looked small. I wanted to shake her awake.

"Oh, you know," she said, and I wondered why she kept crushing her chest, if it made her voice so shaky. "Girls' sweatshirts are too thin and don't do shit to keep you warm. Girl things are just like that. They don't work right. They're just there to—you know. Look nice. And this. This is just nice, you know? This is a nice sweatshirt."

"Janie," I said.

"Don't," she said, flinching. I wasn't anywhere near her; my hand twitched from across the room and she flinched away from it. I swallowed. My spit was cold.

She took a breath, and I heard it rasp into her lungs without filling them. "Sorry," she said. Her voice was small. Her voice was microscopic. "I'm sorry, I'm sorry, I'm sorry. Do you ever feel like you just can't win?"

Of course I did. I lived in fucking Waldo, Iowa. I went to Waldo High School and didn't play sports. I was not particularly rich in friends. I was poorly endowed in just about every possible area of life. Of course I fucking did.

"Oh, stop that," said Janie, a little closer to normal, which meant that she was annoyed. "I can hear you thinking."

"Stop what?"

"Your poor little white boy nice guy act. Don't be the cliché, Micah. You're better than that."

"Janie," I said. I took another step forward and she took another step back.

"Stop," she said, and I did. She took another breath. "Don't. I'm fine."

It was a lie.

"Tell me what's wrong," I said, and she laughed, or she tried. It didn't matter how many breaths she took to steady herself. She tried to laugh and choked.

"Oh, please. You don't want to know what's wrong, Micah. If you wanted to know, you would have—" She stopped. She blinked, and tilted her head to the ceiling so the tears wouldn't fall out. "What isn't wrong? The world is ending. I'm not even being dramatic. The world is fucking ending. You know that, don't you? That's why you picked apocalypses, isn't it? The bees are dying. The ozone layer has more holes than I do. Some idiot could press the wrong button tomorrow and start a nuclear war. It's just—it's a lot of stuff, Micah. And we can't really change it. Isn't that the worst part? We can't really change any of the stuff that matters. Just think about how much sleep we lost trying to fix stuff no one can ever really fix."

"Um," I said. "I guess?"

Her voice is smaller than I've ever heard it when she says, "What are the odds that you'd ditch Maggie and the dance tonight and do something with me?"

"What?" I ask.

"Do you trust me?"

Of course I trusted her. And of course I would go with her—it wasn't a question. Maggie was cute, but she wasn't Janie.

"Just let me text Maggie," I said. "And I have to change."

She smiled. She crossed the room, finally, and wrapped her arms around me. She smelled like she was burning when I put my head on hers. Sometimes I forgot how small she really was. She barely reached my chin. She looked up and her lips were curved and her eyes were too bright and I—

I nearly kissed her, but didn't.

I nearly told her that it was okay, but didn't.

I nearly said scientists were working pretty hard on the bee problem, but didn't.

I did what I always did. I waited until she moved away, until her eyes were a normal brightness and her breath was regular again, and I waited for her to take my hand and pull me after her.

Her hand was cold and sweating.

"I'm having a bonfire," she said. She reached up to push my glasses back up my nose, and kept her hand on my face. "I have marshmallows. Everyone's coming. You're coming, right?"

I hadn't really planned on it. Janie's "everyone" had little overlap with my "everyone." But she didn't let go of my hand until we were in her car, until she stuck her key in the ignition and looked at me, hard. By then my fingers going white in her fist.

"More than anything," she said.

"More than everything," I replied.

On the night of the bonfire, the air was at odds with itself. The wind hurt and the smell of beer was heavy. The cold was sharp and the smoke kept growing.

People were shouting. People were chasing each other with shots and torches.

Janie was curled against me, and her hair kept making me sneeze. In the morning she would pretend this never happened and I would read too much into it, as always.

"Micah?" she said. Her voice was sudden, hitched, almost a gasp, almost a whisper. "Do you think there are things that can't be fixed?"

The fire was in her eyes. The fire. No one was paying attention to the fire. But it was growing in her eyes, and spitting.

"What do you mean? Do you mean us?"

All of a sudden she was upright. Her tailbone dug into my thigh; I winced and tried to move away, and she wouldn't let me go. "No. Not us. Not ever."

On the night of the bonfire, it rained too late. The water pasted her hair to her neck and shoulders. It soaked through my sweatshirt.

She screamed my name.

She screamed, "Do you hear me? More than anything, Micah. *Anything.*"

On the night of the bonfire, there was a match between my fingers.

This I remember clearly: the match, burning toward my fingertips. I remember the heat on my nails, and then the burning. I remember the flame, teased high by the wind, made clear by the cold.

I remember letting go.

I remember the match falling.

"Everything," I said as it hit the ground.

What a night to forget.

What a night to remember.

The Journal Of Janie Vivian

What do you think happened to Sleeping Beauty's bed?

No, really. I want you to answer.

Do you think she ever slept in it again?

She couldn't get up for a hundred years. She was stuck there, tangled in the covers, crushed into that fucking mattress for a hundred fucking years. She couldn't get up. She wanted to, she fought and kicked and clawed and couldn't get out of that hundred-year nightmare.

Do you really think she could ever fall asleep there again?

before

OCTOBER 11

There are a lot of things people never tell you about sex. They say it's romantic and life changing or whatever, sometimes they even say that there's blood and it hurts. But no one tells you about how heavy he is, or how he leaves the condom on your floor. No one ever tells you about the smell of him, sweat and body and *unfamiliarity*, that never goes away. You can stand under the shower and let it go from scalding to hot to lukewarm to cold to freezing. You can throw your sheets and blankets into the washer and the smell will still seep up from the mattress.

Did you know that? I didn't.

I use an entire bottle of body wash. I scrub until my skin is so numb that I can't feel how cold the water is, and then finally, finally I shut it off. The silence is complete, and I slide onto the floor and just lie there, feet together and hands folded. I think of the time Micah and I went to the cemetery with our fists full of dreams. I think of how wide the sky was.

I lie there and cry until I puke. Then I kneel there and puke until my throat is raw.

Then I turn on the water again and wash it all down the drain, tears puke dreams. I clench my fists tighter and tighter. I *will* use them next time.

Next time?

And—damn. There I go. I'm crying again.

I whisper *fuck* until it loses all meaning, not that it had much in the first place.

I don't really know how long it takes me, but I do peel myself off the shower floor, eventually. I'm dry by then, and I go to my room in the stupid new house that I fucking hate, and I look around. My makeup is spilling out of my underwear drawer. The wall behind my desk is splattered with paint and nail polish and Skarpie. There are rocks everywhere.

My bed is a queen and completely stripped right now, so it's hard not to look at. I do my best.

I look at the mirror instead. I remember every single place where he kissed me—every single one—but they have not burned me; I am still whole. If he's bruised me, the bruises have yet to appear. I'm fine. I'm fine.

I make myself look for another five seconds before I sprint to the bathroom again and puke all over again.

Stop crying.

It's fine. I'm fine. I'm going to be okay.

I just need a plan.

Soul Google: *how to decapitate an angel*

no results

How to burn cut punish the wicked no wait

How to stop them

I can see it now, the color of his soul, behind the cloud cover. It's white. It's white and crawling, it's covered in maggots.

I sit down, flop down, *Come on, limbs, get it together*, we have a job to do. We have to do something. Sit. At the computer—yes, I can do that.

R A P E

I type that into Google.

Followed by:

Lawyers in Waldo IA

Average sentence for rape

What constitutes rape

Statistics of rape

Why are there so many rape victims

Why aren't rapists convicted

What do I do?

What the hell do I do

I should have known. That's basic sixth-grade computer class—you can't find everything on the Internet.

I close the tabs. I clear everything.

And then I grab a fistful of rocks and throw on my jacket. I grab my keys and run down the stairs and I figure that since I don't fall, I'm sober enough to drive. I've probably puked up the vodka anyway. I don't look at the muddy footprints on the carpet or the empty bottles on the breakfast bar. I have to get out of here. I shouldn't have put the sheets in the wash. His smell has gotten all the way through the house. I just need to hold it together for a little while longer.

To be honest, I don't remember driving all that much. I remember the dark going by quickly, much faster than the speed limit, holding my breath for as long as I can, and then I'm in Micah's driveway, out of the car and heading for the door on the back porch, slipping into his pitch-black house and sprinting up the stairs. I am quiet by default. I am small and wincing and I'm still holding my breath.

Micah's room is bright. He sleeps with the window open and the moonlight is streaming and awful. There's a pizza box on top of books on top of binders on top of clean clothes on top of dirty, and I almost cry again because it's unfamiliar too, and his room is never unfamiliar. But then there's Micah, a lump under the covers, and my breath whooshes out. He's slept like that for as long as either of us can remember, with the blanket over his head and all of the sides tucked in. Is it safer? Is that why he sleeps like that?

I creep across the room and perch on the edge of the bed and poke him with a finger. I think the moonlight makes it shakier and paler than it really is, but who knows? "Micah," I whisper. "Micah."

He doesn't move, and I can't stand it anymore. The sobs are rising and my throat is thick and shivering, so I crawl next to him and tug on the blankets. He stirs, he turns, he opens his eyes and blinks up at me.

"Janie?"

His voice is heavy with sleep and my tears spill over. Micah, my Micah.

"What is it?" He tries to sit up, but I'm sitting on the covers and he's tangled, and for a moment it's so ironic and strange that I can't move or answer or see him. "What's wrong? Janie—"

"You're hogging the blankets," I manage, and I crawl in with him before he can say anything else. For a moment he hesitates, but he doesn't ask any more questions. He just scoots to give me room and throws half of the covers onto me, and I drag them over my head and pull his arm around me.

"What," he says. "What—"

"Shhh," I say. His lips are soft on my finger. "Shh, I just want to sleep. That's all. Okay?"

And that's what we do. He holds me and I cry and close my eyes and it's like we're on the boat again, like I never left. That Thursday never turned to Friday and Piper and Wes and Jude and Gonzalo and Jizzy and Ander never came over at all, ever. And it feels so possible, easy, to wish time back to the quarry with all of our secrets spilling out into the water, that I keep rewinding and rewinding time. We are babies, embryos. The blanket is a womb, and we're waiting to be born. The world is waiting, and none of this—not last night, not him, not anything—has happened yet.

And who knows?

Maybe it never will.

"Janie Grace Vivian!"

Micah jumps awake beside me. He groans and blinks and then he sees me, and falls off the bed.

"Jesus," he gasps. "What the hell? What are you—are you crying? What's wrong?"

My dad's voice comes again, louder.

"Shit," I whisper. "Shit shit *shit*." I can see our car parked outside, remember their early morning flight. "Oh god, oh god." If they came here, it means they knew I wasn't at home, which means they've seen the house and the vodka bottles and the mess and everything else and oh god oh god oh god.

Footsteps are coming up the stairs. Micah looks terrified, and I am about to puke again. I'm twisting and tying his blanket into nooses. We turn to look at each other, and then the door bursts open.

"We weren't having sex" is the first thing I say. "I was just sleeping over."

But my father is already red in the face and screaming, and it doesn't matter what I say, it's never mattered, and I understand that now, I understand, so while he shouts about the bottles he found, about how worried he and Mom were to go home and find me gone, how irresponsible I am, how disappointed he was, so on and so forth, loudly enough to shake the entire house and make Micah cower with the covers to his ears, and I twist around and grab a pillow, and I bury my face in it and scream as loudly as I can, and the sound is trapped and I am trapped and also going deaf, and in that moment I realize that the universe does not give a single shit about us.

"What—what's going on here?"

I raise my head to see Micah's dad coming through the doorway, haggard from work. Behind him, my mom, twisting her earring. I put my head back down in the pillow because the sun is too bright and I can't do this right now or ever, I can't, I can't.

"Your son is in bed with Janie," I hear my dad yell. "I told you, Karen, I told you that boy was a horrible influence, I told you this would happen. Janie, go downstairs. Get in the car right now or—"

"Or fucking *what?*" I scream, and everyone flinches and goes still. I'm on my feet, on the bed, the tallest person in the room and also the smallest, shaking so hard that my edges might be blurry. "Or what? You'll ground me? You'll send me to bed without supper? How the fuck is that going to help? How the fuck do you think you're protecting me?"

"Get in the car, Janie, or so help me—"

I'm running. Not to his car but to mine, and I hear them all calling after me, and then I can't hear anything anymore as I tear out of the driveway. I make like the universe and don't give a shit. Not a single one.

My favorite metaphor is "between a rock and a hard place." I also like blind men and elephant, bread and circuses, and shooting the messenger.

My favorite Virginia Woolf quote is "Fear no more." I also like "And I said to the star, consume me," "Art is not a copy of the real world; one of the damn things is enough," and "She was off like a bird, bullet, or arrow, impelled by what desire, shot by whom, at what directed, who could say?"

My favorite class is English, though my highest grade is AP Bio. My favorite fairy tale is "The Little Mermaid," and my least favorite is "Sleeping Beauty." My favorite Skarpie has bite marks on both the cap and the end. My favorite matchbook looks like a tiny copy of *Fahrenheit 451*. My favorite Metaphor rocks are the ones worn smooth by the water. My favorite art project I've done this year is my teapot, even though the spout is too low and looks phallic. My favorite color is red, my favorite season is fall, my favorite food is shrimp, my favorite band is Florence + the Machine.

Something else they don't tell you about sex is that it doesn't change you. Your favorite things are still your favorite things. Isn't that strange? It can be such a small thing if you want it to be. I wanted it to be.

But if I move too suddenly, it hurts and I still get whiffs of him. How is that possible? But it is.

I go through the list again and again. My favorite metaphor is "between a rock and a hard place." My favorite

Virginia Woolf quote is "Fear no more." My favorite class is English, my favorite fairy tale is "The Little Mermaid," my favorite Metaphor rocks are smooth.

I really did like him.

I liked him a lot. I liked that his favorite book is *Hatchet* by Gary Paulsen, even though it's probably because he hasn't read anything since fourth grade. I liked that his favorite sport to watch was soccer even though he was a wrestler, I liked the way he wore dark V-necks that hugged his arms, I liked the way his eyelashes curled naturally, I liked the way he always stretched out when he really laughed.

We knew each other to our fingertips. No, that's not right. We only knew each other in our fingertips, and that was nothing at all, and for a while that was okay. We could have been a love story, a fairy tale, an indie film about high school and selective insanity featuring a boy of angel parts and a girl made of dreaming. We could have been all of the best things: bracelets sliding down arms while shots slid down throats, laughter and crashing music in dark and flashing rooms, kisses that started hesitant but didn't stay that way.

We could have cropped out the part where I didn't like his alcohol and hated his music and wanted the kisses to stay soft. We could have deleted the parts no

one wants to see. We could have stopped. We could have
stopped.

Hello, Metaphor.

You are. You are getting smaller.

I'm almost gone too.

There never was a third reason that I named it The
Metaphor. I just didn't want to end at two reasons. I wanted
Micah to pretend with me, back then and now, that this
was the center of the universe, where it started and where it
would end. There's no metaphor here, and soon there won't
be a Metaphor either.

I sit there and stare at it for ages and ages, until the sun
is high in the sky. It brightens and burns and something
inside me splinters. My hands are full of stones and I'm
winding up when Micah catches my arm from behind. I
know it's him before he even touches me, and by then I'm
already turning to sob into his jacket.

We stand like that for a long time.

"It's like half the size it should be," I say into his chest,
muffled and wet.

"Yeah," he says quietly. "They're grinding it into gravel
and using it for the roads. They voted on it a few weeks
ago. That's what my dad said, anyway."

I look up at Micah. His eyes are wide and tired, and

he stands like he doesn't know what to do, doesn't really belong here or there or anywhere. And there, there it is— that's the real reason that we are *us*—because the earth is really just a bunch of body holes waiting to be filled, and neither of us can ever find a place to fit except with each other.

"Why aren't you more worried?" I ask.

He ducks his head and shrugs, but his shoulders don't go all the way down. He scrunches, he's always scrunched and apologetic. My Micah. Mine. "Are you worried? Won't you do something to stop it?"

He makes it sound so easy, but I'm so tired. I'm tired down to my marrow.

I lean against him. Or really—I fall, and he catches me, and I nestle against him and stare at the shrinking Metaphor.

"Maybe we aren't one soul after all," I say, and it's even more terrifying out loud.

His hands fall to his sides, his fingers curling awkwardly and uncurling more awkwardly. He never did know what to do with his hands. They always seemed a bit floppier than hands should be, like there's a bone missing, the common- sense bone that tells you what to do with your hands.

"Oh," he says.

His sadness is everything. He tries to hide it, like he

can hide anything from me, but of course I catch how his breath hitches, the way he stiffens and the way his eyebrows flicker, the way his nostrils widen to suck in a little more air than he would otherwise need. I reach for his hands. I take his awkward fingers and wrap them in my own.

"Maybe I don't have a soul at all," I say.

He relaxes. Immediately, he unwinds against me.

"Well," he says. "You are a ginger."

"Maybe I have a ghost."

"A ghost," he repeats dumbly.

"A ghost," I confirm, but I don't elaborate. I'm too tired to think it through. I don't know what first made me think it, but it sounds right out loud. I don't have a soul at all.

I lean my head back against his shoulder and cross my arms, still holding his hands so that his arms come around me. "You were never in love with me, you know."

His hands immediately start sweating in mine. His chin fits on top of my head and I feel his throat bob along the back of my skull as he swallows, and it's kind of comforting. "That's not true," he says quietly. "You don't get to say that. Look, Janie. We don't have to talk about whatever happened. I won't even ask, if you want. But god, Janie, if you don't think that—that I don't—"

"You don't," I say. I press myself against him, hard, so

that his heartbeat bleeds into my body and shakes my spine. "What if you never knew me, Micah? Not really. You love the dreamer and the painter and the ninja who used to jump through your window. What if that girl isn't real? Then what? You don't love the bitch. You've never even met her."

He laughs a low laugh that I feel everywhere. He leans his face into my hair, so that I feel the shapes of his lips when he says, "Trust me, Janie, I have."

I don't argue, but I just don't think that's true.

after

DECEMBER 6

"Micah? Micah, are you with me?"

"I'm with you," I say. I think I say. "Where are you?"

Someone sighs. Lately there is always someone sighing around me. The lights are bright, the harsh kind of bright. The lights are spinning but nothing else; nothing is spinning but everything is wobbling.

"Can I go to sleep now?" I ask, and I don't hear the answer.

Janie Vivian is dead.

When I woke up in the hospital on the day after the bonfire, the first thing I asked Dewey was if she was there. I remember that now. My head hurt because it had split open when Dewey punched me and I hit the ground, but I didn't know that. I didn't remember anything after the day she moved.

It was still raining outside and I wanted to know if I could see her. If she was on the same floor as me. Dewey told me that she wasn't. Eventually, eventually it came out that she was in the morgue, and the world exploded and rebuilt itself without that particular detail.

The doctors, the nurses telling me again. I remember, and it hurts. I remember how apocalyptically it hurt every time, every single time, they told me she was dead. Janie Vivian is dead. I remember my dad, sitting beside me and saying in his quiet voice that on the night of the bonfire, Janie Vivian fell into the quarry and never came back out. They kept telling me and I kept forgetting.

Eventually they stopped trying. I could understand a world where she was in Nepal, though I couldn't figure out why she didn't text me back. I could understand a world where she was distant but not lost. I couldn't understand a world without her.

I remember forgetting.

And there's more.

God, there's so much more.

"Dewey? Oh, fuck, Dewey. Dewey."

"Yeah, I'm here. Micah, it's fine. It's gonna be fine, we're going to the hospital. We're in an ambulance because you're too fucking tall to carry. You idiot. It's going to be fine."

"Dewey, the fire."

"Uh, let's talk about the fire later. Go to sleep. No, wait. Shit, don't listen to me. Don't go to sleep. Are you listening? Micah. Stay awake. We're going to the hospital, okay?"

"No. No, no no, I don't want to go to the hospital again. I don't want to, I don't want to. Oh, god, Dewey, do they think I set the fire?"

"It doesn't matter right now, just shut the hell up—"

"Dewey, I remember. I'm starting to remember. I remember that Janie's dead. Oh, god, she's dead. She drowned. You kept telling me about it."

"Yeah, you kept forgetting. You're really fucked up, okay? Just take it easy."

"But I remember the fire too."

"Micah, don't—"

"I remember the match. Dewey, I remember dropping the match. Did I tell you about that? They think I set the fire, and I remember a match. I just don't remember when. I don't."

"Micah—"

"But I wouldn't do that. I wouldn't burn down her house. Why would I do that? I wouldn't do that, but what if I did? Did I?"

"Micah, *shut your fucking mouth.*"

~

The memories do not return so much as plunge. Shatter back into place.

My dad in a suit, his tie too tight. Checking on me before he goes to her funeral.

Yellow flowers in the school, everywhere and dying.

People carrying stones in their pockets. Writing Virginia Woolf quotes on their arms.

The notes people wrote for her and taped to the wall in the cafeteria. The way the soup splattered across them when Ander pushed me.

Understanding, however briefly, that she was dead. Heading to the quarry to see where the water climbed or she slid, forgetting she drowned halfway there.

Forgetting was the easy part. Remembering is harder, but not as apocalyptically
  painful
  as knowing that there is more to come.

The Journal Of Janie Vivian

~~Morrow and Lietrich Law Offices~~
~~920 Niagara Road~~
~~Waldo, IA 50615~~
~~(319) 555-8372~~

~~Ghomp Schumacher Krumke LLP~~
~~34 Main Street~~
~~Waldo, IA 50615~~
~~(319) 555-3854~~

~~Kirk Olsen, Attorney at Law~~
~~4300 North 14th Street~~
~~Cedar Falls, IA 50613~~
~~(319) 555-0770~~

~~Joshing and Jones LLP~~
~~275 South Bend Boulevard~~
~~Des Moines, IA 50301~~
~~(515) 555-2861~~

before

OCTOBER 13

I wait in Micah's car until 7:57, even though we arrive at 7:35 and he gives up asking me why I won't just go in and leaves at 7:40. I huddle in the passenger seat with my arms around my knees. At 7:57, I untangle myself and sprint for the school. You would think that the hallways would be mostly empty by then, but nope, good job, Janie, way to plan. *Everyone* is in the halls, rushing and pushing and squeezing, and I know they're not staring at me but just . . . I wish the halls were empty. I don't want to touch any of them.

I walk into Mr. Markus's room. I go to my seat, next to Ander.

Right next to him.

I sit down. I cross my legs and fold my arms into knots.

He's sprawled, spilling over the side of his desk and his legs spread wide open and just everywhere, and I can feel his heat, I can hear his breathing. I sit and I hold my breath as long as I can, and when I can't, I'm gasping, I can smell it. I can smell his maggot soul.

I might puke. I might run. I might explode and cover the room with Janie guts.

But I will not fucking cry.

He will never, ever, ever make me cry again.

I decided that this morning while getting ready for school in Micah's basement. (Which was totally a fun arrangement, by the way. Much better than my brilliant plan of sleeping by the Metaphor. There was this little ledge out of the wind under the bridge, and there was something almost romantic about that: sleeping under the stars, just me and the world and hypothermia. I would have done it. I'm never living with my parents again.)

I don't know how he explained it to his dad. He dragged me back to his house after my meltdown at the Metaphor. He and his dad chatted for a minute while I sat in the other room and picked at my nails, and then Mr. Carter poked his head in said hi and waved his awkward, common-sense-boneless hand and asked me if I needed anything, and I said no, and he left for his shift at Pick 'n Save and Micah and I watched more cartoons under an afghan his grandmother made him.

Ander turns. He's looking at me. His maple syrup eyes

are wrapping me in webs of sap. I look around for Piper, quick, words, talk to someone, look away, but she's not in the seat next to me.

No, she's not there. She's all the way across the room with a Starbucks cup in her hand.

And. She. Didn't. Bring. Me. One.

"All right," Mr. Markus says from his desk. "Well, as the three people who utilize the English Twelve website will know, today was supposed to be a peer review day for the first draft of your thesis papers, but seeing as the same three people are the only ones who have sent me drafts, this is clearly not going to happen." He sighs, a long sigh that carries all of the disappointment in the world that I have not already staked out for myself. "Well? Get laptops. Write."

I don't. I pull out my journal and start paging through. In there, in bits and pieces, spread across pages and pages, are my fractured fairy tale autobiography and a mostly done paper about fairy tale miracles with all of my sketches of universes and oceans and heart variations.

Miracles, one of them begins, *do not belong to religions. Miracles belong to the desperate, which is why every religion, every philosophy, and most importantly, every fairy tale always has a moment of salvation, a eureka, an enlightenment. We are all chasing and chasing tails, running and running in circles, until a wolf or the witch or the stepmother jumps out and trips us, and we fall flat,* splat, *and we lie bare and bleeding and breathless and finally, finally look and see whatever it is—salvation or eureka or enlightenment or a hunter or a prince or a glass slipper—in front of us. And that's what miracles are. Not solutions, but catalysts. Not answers, but chances.*

Forget fairy tales. Screw Andersen and Grimm and Perrault—I could have built a thousand pairs of wings out of this beautiful bullshit.

I open my journal to a new page. I write *THESIS* at the top and underline it three times for emphasis and a fourth for luck, out of habit. I start again.

Miracles do not belong to fairy tales. Miracles belong to the desperate, because only the desperate believe in bullshit.

There.

End thesis. I expect my Pulitzer any day now.

Ander is still watching me.

It's all so familiar, and I am even wearing the same shoes.

My hand shoots into the air. Every single person in the room looks at me, except Mr. Markus.

I cough. He doesn't look up. "Mr. Markus," I finally say. Whisper, more like. *Come on, voice. Pull it together.* "Can I go to the bathroom?"

He nods without looking up from his grading. I grab my stuff and head for the door.

Behind me, someone mutters, "Pregnancy test, Janie?"

It's Ander. I know it's Ander.

I don't look back. I pause at the bathroom and wonder if I *do* need a pregnancy test, but no, don't think about that, I will not fucking cry I will not I will not.

I go to the art room instead. I go to my senior studio closet and I look around. And then I explode.

Here is what Janie guts look like: broken charcoal pencils and empty glaze jars on the floor. And paper, paper everywhere, shredded feathers and scraps of plans. A broken teapot that doesn't need a fucking lid. Shattered clay map of a shattered world. Greenware bowls smashed to dust.

And one clay covered in lucky pentagrams and Viking runes and witch-curse-repelling spells that I throw against the wall as hard as I can, so hard, so hard that it doesn't shatter, it doesn't crumble, it dissolves. It turns to dust and I sink into it and close my eyes.

I leave the wings alone.

I have to finish the wings.

I have to finish something.

I roll over and push my hair out of my face.

Just one miracle.

I go to lunch because I'm hungry. I'm hungry and I want to eat and they can't stop me with their bent heads and whispers and staring. I can do what I want. I can do whatever I want.

Even the lunch lady stares at me. She forgets to give me a cookie.

By the time I get to the table, I don't have energy to sit. I collapse. I am a bag of bones, and I have been robbed of my spinal cord. They were talking about homecoming and dresses and dinner reservations, but they stopped when I was five feet away.

"Hey," I say, and look around. "Where's Piper?"

A beat too long of silence. Then, finally, Katie says, "She went home. Cramps."

"Okay, Janie," Carrie Lang says. Her long hair droops onto the table as she leans toward me. "What happened? What's this? Is it Ander?"

Karma. Karma, I knew you were real. I knew filling Carrie's lawn with balloons was an investment in the future.

"Is it true that you guys had sex and then you dumped him because he sucked?" she asks, and adds, "Not the good kind, obviously."

Blink. Blink again. "Wait. What?"

"Is that what this is?" she asks. "Janie, you know you could have called us. That was your first time, right? Babe, you should have *called me*. Is it because it hurt a lot? Or was he really just that bad?"

"What did he say?"

"Ander? I don't know, he didn't text me back. But Jizzy said that you guys did it and then you freaked and dumped him. God, Janie, I can't believe you didn't call me!"

"He was tiny, wasn't he," Blair says, taking a teensy-teensy bite of her salad. "I knew it. The hot ones are always falsely advertised. I keep telling you guys that."

They're all leaning in now, Blair and Sadie and Kelsey and Meredith. They blink their big, big eyes and wait for me to tell them all about Ander and me. Ander and Janie.

No.

I imagine sketching the scene: me and an oversized hammer, off-balance and smashing, their Whac-A-Mole heads popping like cherries.

I want to say something, something scathing and brilliant and conversation ending, but let's talk false advertising. The real picture would look something like this: them and their mole eyes and twitching noses, me with my guts back in my art room and my brain melting out onto my lunch tray and my mouth catching all the flies that buzz around the trash can. And I know then that I did the right thing when I crossed out those lawyer numbers. Who the fuck would take my side? No one in Waldo. No one here. No one who saw me scuttling after him since freshman year, flirting at every chance, kissing at regionals. Kissing kissing kissing.

I close my mouth and open it again and close it again, and in the end I just take my tray and walk away. I briefly consider the bathroom, but, ugh, who could actually eat lunch in a school bathroom outside of a nineties chick flick? Gross. I can barely walk through the door without gagging.

Hello, universe. I know you don't give a shit. But you handed me the wrong nineties chick flick.

I don't want this one.

I don't freaking want it.

I just can't stay at this table. I can't breathe.

But—there! There's Micah! And Dewey! I'm even glad to see Dewey! I didn't know they ate lunch in the hallway! Okay, I totally did. But I pretend I didn't as I walk over. I pretend and pretend and pretend.

"Look, I'm just saying," Dewey is saying as I get closer, "that's *who she is*. Hell, she's been—*that* for so long that she probably doesn't even fucking remember what the truth is. She didn't fucking change, Micah. The two of you are just so goddamn parasitic that you can't even see it. Get your head out of your ass. Just because she flirts with you doesn't mean you stand a chance. She flirts with everyone."

Quick, can I get away? No, Micah has already spotted

me. His cheeks go red so fast it's almost funny. My breath catches a little, but I force it out.

I drop my tray next to Dewey and say, "I don't flirt with you."

"Yeah, well, there's that whole thing about me not being into girls," he says. He doesn't even try to look embarrassed about seeing me. He takes another bite of pizza before he talks again, and not to me. "Do whatever you want, dude. But I'll be waiting with the I TOLD YOU SO sign when she fucks you over again."

Metaphorical sign, I tell myself. They don't have a real sign.

Do they?

"Shut up," Micah mutters. He doesn't look at me. Why doesn't he look at me? I prod him with my soul. He still doesn't look up. But he does talk in my direction. "What are you doing here?"

"She's here because no one back in there wants to sit with her," Dewey says. Does he always chew with his mouth open? Pepperoni pieces and wet pizza dough between his gnashing, gnashing teeth. "Same reason we're out here. Right? Cameron's been telling everyone that he dumped you because you had sex and then you shouted rape because you regretted it in the morning. That true?" He looks straight at me.

I didn't exactly *mean* to dump my lunch tray over his head.

"Fuck you," I say. My voice is perfect—so cold, so wonderfully hollow. "Get a life, Dewey, and stop chasing Micah around. He doesn't love you back."

He loves *me*.

Then I walk away. Just kidding. I sprint the hell out of there. I go straight to the parking lot, and I dig out my phone and start Googling directions on hot-wiring a car. Micah can find another ride home. I'm stealing his.

I'm scrolling through the Wikipedia page, holding my breath because I just have to keep it together until I'm in the car driving away, when suddenly—

"Janie."

I yelp and drop my phone and close my eyes and take a moment to tell my heart to *freaking chill*, because it's not Ander and it's not Dewey, it's just Micah. Just Micah.

He bends down to get my phone, and his eyebrows furrow. "You were gonna steal my car?"

"Yeah." I sigh. "but it's a lot more complicated than nineties chick flicks would have you believe."

"No shit," he says, and gets in the car. "Come on."

I slide into the passenger side. "Metaphor?"

"Sure."

We drive in silence. I study my palms. There are four

perfect half moons where my nails dug in, and a fate line that looks normal. Perfectly straight, average length. I used to think that destiny was fluid, because isn't that the point of every Disney movie and Saturday-morning cartoon? You make your own choices. You decide how life goes. I always thought that your fate line would change if something happened, *bam*, something goes wrong and the line on your palm goes all wonky to reflect that. Nope. It still looks fine.

Well, fuck you too, fate.

I dig my nails into my palms again and look ahead. Staring contest, glaring contest. Let's go, universe. You and me, right here, right now.

Micah pulls to a stop farther away than normal, and the Metaphor looks even smaller. I get out of the car. *Slam.* He closes his door as quietly as he can, as if that'll make my slam less offensive. I shove my hands into my pockets and start toward the quarry, and he follows, and we stop right at the edge of the rocks. I don't even need to tilt my head back to squint at the top anymore.

"You know," I finally say, "it's actually really fucking ugly."

"Yeah, I guess," says Micah.

"It's really just a pile of shit."

But Micah isn't looking at the Metaphor anymore, he's

looking at me. His eyes are all wide and worried, and he says my name, and I look at the sky and wonder, *How many times can a person explode?*

Here's some metaphorical resonance for you: I don't want to look up at the Metaphor anymore. You should not look up to shit. You should not want to fucking climb to the top of something that shouldn't even exist, and this isn't how I wanted to reach the top anyway. I wanted to reach the top of a mountain. This is barely a pile anymore. It's a disappearing heap of rejected rocks that should have drowned with the rest of the quarry.

"Janie, what are you—Janie, what the hell? Janie, stop, Janie—"

I dig my hands in and I pull. I grab, I throw, I kick, I plunge again and again and I swear, I swear, I fucking swear, I will tear this thing to the ground.

I don't know when I started crying, but I don't care anymore, I don't care that I can't stop, I don't care that I can't see. I don't need to see. I just need to get rid of it. I need to break it apart. I need—I need—

And then Micah is pulling me away and I might be screaming, a whirlwind, limbs and fists and bursting, but this time he knows exactly what to do with his arms, and they're around me. My face is in his coat and his coat smells like Dewey's cigarettes and rain and maybe a little bit like pot, but mostly it smells like him, like wood polish and honeycomb and mine.

"God," I blubber into him. "God damn it all, Micah."

He puts his chin on top of my chin. "What's wrong?" he asks quietly. "Tell me what's wrong."

"No," I sob. Because what's the point?

And that's the thing about Micah. He leaves it at that.

after

DECEMBER 15

Court-mandated alcohol therapy is not the worst sentence for underage drinking. As far as hearings go, mine is easy. They just send me back to Dr. Taser for a few more sessions.

Dr. Taser says that now that I have started to remember, I can start to heal too. This is bullshit, because this is not the first time I've pushed crap completely out of my mind.

"My father picked my first name for his father and my mom picked my middle name for her favorite month," I told her last time I was here. "She died when I was three years old, and I don't remember her at all. I should, but I don't. You're supposed to start remembering shit when you're, what, two?"

"Language, Micah," Dr. Taser said gently.

"Yeah, sorry. So my mom died in this car accident. There had been, like, an ice storm the day before or something, and she wanted to check on my grandparents, and she was going to spend the day there, right? And my dad was having this affair with some lady who lived in the neighborhood. She used to make us lemon bars. These, like, really fantastic lemon bars, right? So while my mom was dying, he was having sex with some lady down the street and I was with my babysitter, who also lived down the street. And when they called him from the hospital, he didn't answer because his phone was downstairs and he was upstairs having sex—yeah, okay, you get it. So he finishes what I hope was damn good sex, it better have been fucking worth it—"

"Micah—"

"—and hears that his wife is dead, and he never gets over it. He picks us up and moves us to Waldo. And he tells me all of this in, like, third grade. A confession or whatever, like that'll fix his shit, and I just . . . I don't know. The next day, I forgot about it. And he kept telling me and telling me and I kept forgetting. I don't remember when I finally started remembering what really happened to him and Mom. I stopped talking to him when I did, though. It's not like I had that much to say to him before, anyway. But fuck, I know I should care, but I don't. So, yeah, that's me. Oh, and I feel fine now. This therapy is really helping."

Today is the last time I have to be here. I have paid the

money I owe the government for harming my body with more than fourteen drinks per week, I have gone to the therapy sessions, I have nodded and agreed to be responsible from now on. I go to Dr. Taser's office, where she is already waiting with her iPad.

"Can I get you anything?" she asks me. "Water? Coffee?"

"The hell out of here," I say, and smile as if I were joking. I'm unconvincing and she's not convinced, but what the hell. We both keep smiling.

"Sorry," I say. "Tons of strain."

Dr. Taser nods sympathetically. "Do you feel more like talking about Janie today? Maybe we can try a happy memory again?"

I look up. Her eyes are dark, her head is cocked, her posture as welcoming as posture can be. I ask her, "You ever dissect a sheep heart?"

She looks startled, but I plow on. "I haven't either. We were supposed to for Anatomy and Physiology, but— well. It doesn't matter, I never wanted to. I took the class because Janie was taking it. Anyway, I did the dissection online today, and there was this picture of a human heart without fat or muscle in the introduction to the lab. It was just the veins."

"And you wish Janie could have seen it?" asks Dr. Taser, typing away on her iPad.

"She already saw it," I say, and both Dr. Taser and Janie frown at me. "She saw it in seventh grade at Lorraine Bay National Park."

I told her about us, about that day. Ander Cameron's mom had been our chaperone. She had been a decent person. She brought us cookies. Not sure what happened to Ander. Anyway, we collected rock samples and dirt samples and identified plants and shit, and then we had lunch on this big hill. Janie had Lunchables, the nacho kind that came with a candy bar for dessert. I remember because I was jealous. My dad packed me a hot ham sandwich that wasn't supposed to be hot. Afterward, everyone started rolling down the hill. Dewey dragged me into it, but it actually really hurt—it wasn't, like, some groomed country club hill. There were trees. There were branches sticking up and bugs under rotting leaves and poison ivy. So eventually Dewey ditched me, which he always seemed to do, and I sat at the top of the hill and looked up.

"What are you doing?"

I jumped when Janie plopped down next to me, and then I looked around. "No one's paying attention," Janie said by way of explanation. "They're too busy rubbing themselves in poison ivy. I hope Robbie gets it on his dick."

She and Robbie had just broken up. God, I just remember looking over at her, looking and wondering how she did it, how she was so damn comfortable. We'd just watched the sex video thing the week before, and Mr. Endero made us say *penis* three times without laughing to get into the room. I told Janie about it later, and she looked at me straight in the eye and said, "Penis. Penis. Penis. Grow up, Micah."

I could not. So maybe that was why she started leaving me behind.

"So?" said Janie. "What are we looking at?"

Just the sky, really. Above there were only tangles of branches and the sky. And I was about to tell her that when she spread her arms and took a deep breath.

"Oh," she whispered, and I didn't need to look up anymore. "I see. I feel it now, Micah. Like the sky is falling down. It makes my lungs hurt. The sky is falling down and my breath is too small to hold the air. Micah—you feel it? The world is growing bigger. I can feel it."

Then she fell back. The ground thudded and I was freaked, because she said the world was growing bigger, and I thought it would swallow her. Pull her away.

But it didn't. We just kept staring at the sky and we didn't get poison ivy.

"The sheep heart looked just like that," I tell Dr. Taser. "The trees."

"That does sound like a happy memory," she says,

sounding pleased for the first time. It's not happy, really, because Janie doesn't know that the trees looked like a heart and she never will because she's never going to do the dissection because she's dead and buried and I still don't remember most of how that happened. But what a nice note to end on.

I shrug. "I guess. I went back to the bus after that."

She blinks. "Why?"

"She wanted me to. We were never supposed to talk to each other in public—people stopped rolling down the hill and so I had to go. I left her. That's what friends do."

But that's not what friends do, and Dr. Taser hands me her iPad to Google *friendship* to prove it. She pushes a notebook into my hands and tells me that it'll help to write down what I remember. And then, finally, she lets me leave.

In the waiting room, I sit on the couch and wait for Dewey. My license is still suspended and my dad is at work, but Dewey offered to give me a ride, presumably because he's the reason I'm here.

"Hey," he greets me as he pulls up in front. "You get your head fixed? Ready to drink responsibly?"

"Screwed on all the way and ready to be deadened by alcohol," I say, climbing into the passenger seat, "which I feel like you owe me."

"I'm out of Canadian, but got the cheapest whiskey in Iowa in the trunk. Just . . . take it easy, okay?"

"Janie's dead," I tell him.

He keeps his eyes on the road. "You've mentioned."

"I remember the bonfire," I say. I stare at the backs of my hands, going finger to finger, counting. "The bonfire. I remember most of what happened before, I think. The week of is still fuzzy, but I remember the Metaphor disappearing. God, she was pissed."

I stop then and wait for Janie to say something, but she's gone too.

"Our birthday, her wings. But the bonfire, Dewey. That night, at her house. What the hell happened?"

He stares at the road. I stare at him.

"We fought," I say slowly. "You punched me. Did that happen?"

Dewey doesn't answer for so long that I almost take his silence as a no. But finally he looks away from the road and leans his head on the wheel, and I should be more worried than I am. "Yeah," he says. I barely hear him.

I stare at him until he lifts his head from the wheel and steers the car back into the right lane.

Everyone has secrets, Janie told me once. "Ours are just bigger than everyone else's."

Maybe she was wrong.

"Dewey," I say. "You have whiskey?"

He nods, and then sighs. "You're still doing it."

Presumably we go back to my house and play Metatron: Sands of Time and drink then, but I don't remember any of it. The next morning we have massive hangovers and an empty bottle of whiskey, but to our credit, neither of us left.

THe JouRNAL OF Janie Vivian

Once upon a time, there was a princess who didn't get saved. I don't really know what to tell you about her because her story was never written down. Maybe the dragon ate her. Maybe the prince just never got around to rescuing her. No one wants to read that fairy tale, so no one wrote it.

Or maybe the truth is that no princesses get rescued, ever. Maybe there are no happily ever afters, not really.

before

Mr. Markus held me after class today to ask why the paper I submitted was nothing like my proposal. He probably also wanted to know why it was only nineteen words long, but I didn't have a good reason for either.

"This isn't the project you proposed," he tells me. "This isn't even a thesis."

"You said it was an adaptable project," I remind him. "Don't you want it to evolve organically?"

"You still owe me an autobiography," he reminds me. "Will I be seeing your fractured fairy tales anytime soon?"

"Probably not," I say. "They're not very exciting. They're kind of pathetic, actually."

He pushes the paper aside and clears the desk so there's nothing between us. He folds his hands. "How are the wings coming along, Janie?"

The wings.

Oh, the wings.

Actually, they're beautiful. They're not finished, not even close, but they're beautiful. I've cut through a volume each of Grimm and Andersen, and I'm starting on Perrault. It's a much slower process when I do it alone because I always want to read each page before I cut it up. The wings themselves are in the art studio, and only one side is full of feathers. They're beautiful, but it's going to take a miracle to finish them.

I just keep getting distracted by the fairy tales, reading them once upon a time to happily ever after, and it's hard because I'm not finding many miracles anymore. There's a lot of people who never get saved. There are a lot of people who get toes or heels cut off, who are stuffed in barrels studded with nails and rolled down hills, who are cursed or burned alive or forgotten. Guess how many of them are women.

(Lots.)

"They're coming along" is all I say. I pick at my nails. I've never been much of a nail biter, but they're pretty mangled at the moment.

"Janie," Mr. Markus says in his sandpaper voice. "What do you need?"

I almost cry.

So many people have asked me if I'm okay without really

wanting an answer, or they ask if they can do anything without meaning it. Carrie and Micah and the girls at our lunch table when I pass them in the halls with my face permanently red from holding my breath. No one has asked me what I need. Not even Micah.

There are a lot of things I'd like. I wish my parents would help me and I wish I hadn't taken those last couple of shots. I wish I had been born with endings, I wish I had been born with good ones, I wish I could finish the wings, I wish I never had to see Ander again, I wish the Metaphor wasn't disappearing. I want time to pass faster and I want it to stop altogether, but need? Need is a very different question.

"I need to know the key to happiness," I say. "I can't wait until graduation. I need to know now."

For a second I think he's going to refuse. But then he leans back in his creaky swivel chair and folds his hands over his stomach. "I didn't plan on being a teacher," he says.

I wait.

"I was going to be a stockbroker."

For a second I am quiet. And then I sigh. "Really? This is the key to happiness? The world really is made of disappointment, isn't it."

He laughs.

Mr. Markus has an amazing laugh—it's a full-body experience. He throws back his head and you see the air move through him, and for a moment, I thought, *That's it.* That's the key to happiness.

"I finished business school, and I was getting ready to move to New York. I had a job lined up, and the van was packed. I was ready to catch my plane when the mover stopped me."

"Why?"

"He told me not to tip him," Mr. Markus said. "He told me that money probably couldn't buy happiness, but I'd need all I could get to try, because I was going to be miserable for the rest of my life. Then he drove off with the van, and I drove in the direction of the airport, but I didn't take the exit. I kept driving."

We sat there in silence for a solid minute.

"I don't get it," I finally said. "And what happened to all your furniture?"

"I have no idea," Mr. Markus says. "But happiness is a choice. That's the key. A choice."

Is it, though? Is it really? Maybe.

Maybe, for the lucky ones.

I am not one of the lucky ones. I can fill my pockets with stones and mark myself everywhere and set the entire universe on fire, but it's not going to change anything. I am not one of the lucky ones.

So here is what the unlucky ones choose between: prude or slut. Angel or devil. Maybe *choice* isn't the right word—you're always one or the other.

Damsel or villainess. That's what it comes down to.

I guess the question that really matters is: which one gets the real happy ending?

after

The journal I start is not like hers. There are no magazine cutouts and collages and sketches, there are no plans, there are no promises. There are lists. Words. Sounds. Anything I can remember. Anything that might be real.

Most of them make no sense, or not enough of it. Dewey, punching me. Water, rising. Fire, fire, fire.

I'm failing online school. I spend all day sitting at my desk staring at the journal and trying, trying to put it all back in place.

I write everything down, but most of it doesn't help much.

Rumor is they're just waiting on the arson analysis to arrest me. No one tells me anything.

I would say that I wish I cared more, but that is false.

In my journal, I write.

Carrie Lang's yard. Balloons. Caleb Matthers not in school next day—hives. Allergic to latex.

Janie and Ander flirting across the room. Him looking at her journal and her face going cold.

The apocalypse. Music.

Wrestling. Ander pummeled.

The note on my bed that smelled like coffee. Adults in a tiny-ass boat.

Metaphor disappearing.

Janie in my sweatshirt.

Piper running and crying.

The bonfire. More than one?

Janie's wings.

I had a match.

Why did I have a match?

Water, fire.

What happened to Janie Vivian?

Why.

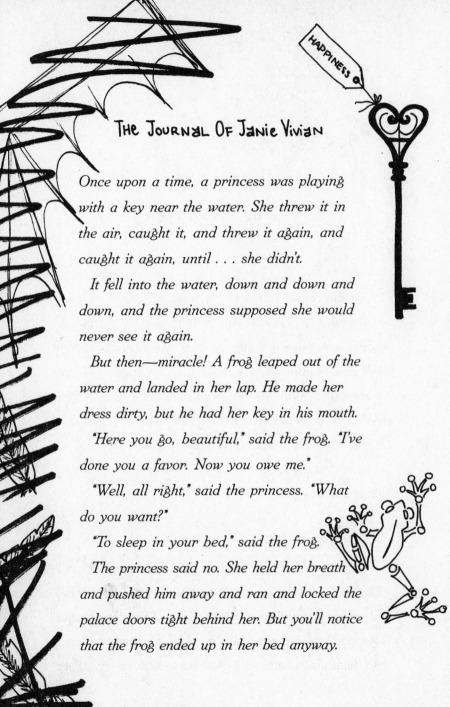

The Journal Of Janie Vivian

Once upon a time, a princess was playing with a key near the water. She threw it in the air, caught it, and threw it again, and caught it again, until . . . she didn't.

It fell into the water, down and down and down, and the princess supposed she would never see it again.

But then—miracle! A frog leaped out of the water and landed in her lap. He made her dress dirty, but he had her key in his mouth.

"Here you go, beautiful," said the frog. "I've done you a favor. Now you owe me."

"Well, all right," said the princess. "What do you want?"

"To sleep in your bed," said the frog.

The princess said no. She held her breath and pushed him away and ran and locked the palace doors tight behind her. But you'll notice that the frog ended up in her bed anyway.

before

OCTOBER 16

Please direct your attention to phase ten, step thirteen: candygrams. Ander was supposed to ask me (*again*—he should have asked me already, but I would have made it very clear to him that I wanted a confirmation) with one of the candygrams that the student council sells to raise money for the dance. It was supposed to be delivered during seventh hour, and the whole class was supposed to watch as I said yes.

Can you imagine?

Yes.

I don't get a candygram from Ander.

I *do* get thirty or so from his friends. They come in a pile during calc. It's enough candy to make all of my teeth fall out, lollipop after heart-shaped lollipop. I unwrap one and sweep the rest into my backpack while everyone watches. I bite the heart in half and look them each in the eye. They all look away, one by one. All because I shouted rape. Funny, right? Because I *didn't*. I didn't, but Wes and Ander tell everyone I did. I decided not to shout anything at all but everyone in school still knows I had sex with Ander, and who the hell would ever believe that I didn't want to, right?

The note that accompanies the lollipop I unwrap says *Janie Vivian is a whore, Janie Vivian is a bore, Janie Vivian has no friends, Janie Vivian needs to end.*

Isn't that cute?

I think it's adorable.

Senior homecoming. My dress is covered in sequins and incredibly short. My shoes are five-inch stilettos and I was going to paint my nails red. I was going to be beautiful—devastatingly, truly, madly. I'm returning all of it tomorrow morning.

Micah is going with Maggie Morgenstern, who isn't even close to good enough for him even though he won't believe me. She's a sophomore and I guess she's cute enough. He asked if I wanted to go with them, but he doesn't really want me there. Still, I guess it's sweet. He comes by my locker to make sure I'll be okay working on the wings here alone. Stupid, silly, lovely Micah, who is still oblivious. The rumors are out there, if he'd care to listen. "Tell me what's wrong," he says sometimes, so quietly that it's almost not out loud at all. He doesn't really want to know. That's the truth. If he really wanted to know he would press a little, ask again when I said I didn't want to talk about it. But he doesn't.

So after he and everyone else leaves, I swing my backpack full of lollipops over my shoulder and head to the art studio. I'd already put twelve dozen eggs in Mr. Markus's minifridge and told him it was for my project. He didn't even blink twice.

Originally, I had wanted to smash one in every single locker in the senior hallway, but I guess that isn't fair. The ninjas are nothing if not fair. Egging Waldo High's seniors isn't exactly an effective *fuck you* to society. So instead I go straight to Ander's locker, where I used to wait for him every day after French. I know his combination by heart.

I don't light a match because luck isn't real and I'm not one of the lucky ones, anyway. I just twist the lock and open the door and dump all twelve dozen eggs inside.

I start out one by one, holding them high and dropping them on his textbooks and reveling a little in the way the eggs break in layers—shell, white, yoke. But it's an awful lot of eggs, and by the third dozen, I'm just opening the cartons and pouring them in, waterfalling, everywhere.

I blow it all a kiss, and I'm about to walk away when I see that he still has my picture taped to his locker door. It's the classic senior portrait pose: hair twirl, bright bright smile, oversaturated eyes. At the bottom, in my handwriting, it says, *I'll like you forever, I'll love you for always, xoxo <3.*

Well. That just isn't true.

I rip it off and set it on the eggs. I slam the door. I go back down the hall and close myself in the art room. The janitors cleaned up after I left on Monday. My mess is gone, but there's lots of dust left. It's everywhere.

I sit on the ground and pull the candygrams out of my backpack, along with my journal. I copy them down in Journal Twelve, one per page, to investigate further and figure out a ninja hit list. The Skarpie bleeds everywhere.

Roses are red, violets are blue, Janie's a whore, and a little bitch too.

Slut.

Whore.

Bitch.

Just wanted to get laid. Nice ass, though. I'd be down. You can dump me right afterward and I won't say a word. Not even to Cameron. HMU.

Liar.

Liar.

Liar.

I guess I can't really argue with that.

Once everything is copied down, I smooth out the candygrams. I pull the wings closer and find my scissors and glue, and I start making feathers again. And for a little while, it's okay. It's okay again. It's just me in my closet of a studio with wings that just barely fit, and feathers.

I glue these new ones at the very top of the unfinished left wing, in all directions. They stick up, ugly and messy and uneven, with glue oozing out of the sides, and they don't really cover the bamboo and wire frame, which is already loose.

One wing is perfect, covered with fairy tales. The other unravels. It collapses.

It's dark when I finally leave. Not dark enough to mean that the football game is starting soon, but dark enough that little girls really shouldn't be wandering around alone. Why, that's just asking for it. Duh.

"Janie?"

I think we've established by now that Ander Cameron is a very good wrestler. But on that night, I don't think it mattered so much. I don't think it was that he was strong. I think it was that I was completely paralyzed. I can't breathe. I can't, I can't do it.

I thought it was the vodka, but I'm sober right now, and my bones and blood and marrow are still too heavy to react. My lungs are still broken.

Run? Hide? Fight? What do I do what do I do what do I do? I can't run, because I can't move. There's nothing to hide behind in this hall. Fight? Ha ha. I could curl up and tie myself in knots until he leaves. Turn and kick his balls off his body. Walk, keep walking, and maybe he'll think he's wrong, that it's not me at all, and why not? Who is Janie Vivian?

"Aw, Janie, come on. Wait. Wait, let's talk, okay? Can we please talk?"

His hand. It's on my shoulder. He's touching me.

He pulls me around so we can look at each other. So I can see his pretty, pretty face.

"Hey," says Ander.

Hey, he says.

He bites his lip when I don't say anything, perfect lip and perfect teeth, his eyelashes fluttering like he's worried. And my eyes—

No, don't, eyes. Look. Look at him.

"Listen," he says. He clears his throat, and then he does it again. A big, manly throat clear. "Look, Janie. I just—I just wanted to say . . . um. Look. I'm sorry, okay?"

He's just standing there. Look at that, legs. He's just standing there. If you would just do your freaking job, you could kick him *sofuckinghard* in the balls that he would never stand up again. If you'd just walk that distance, get a little closer, you could make it so he doesn't hurt anyone again, ever.

But I'm pretty useless, honestly. Someone stole my spine.

"Get away from me," I finally whisper. *Getaway-getawaygetaway.*

"Oh, come on, Janie. I'm trying to apologize here, okay? I just—Janie, look, I get it, I was kind of an asshole. But let's face it, you've been a bitch. So let's just call it even? I mean. Look, I already talked to Piper, she won't say anything. We can pretend like it never happened if you want. Janie, come on. I miss you, okay?"

Oh, that's nice. That's—

That's when I kick him in the crotch. As hard as I can, and it's still not enough.

He's on the ground, his hands cupped around his balls, panting, but he's still looking at me, and he—

He grins.

"Fuck," he groans. "Aw, Janie. Okay, I guess I deserve that. We good now?"

I stare at him. Really, that was what I needed. I just needed to know what I was worth. A kick to the crotch, and he thinks we're even.

We fall asleep to fairy tales, and the world rotates and revolves and time passes and we grow up and we understand that they are false. There are not heroes and princesses and villains. It's not that easy.

But I think I unlearned that too well. There are no wicked queens or vengeful sorcerers, but that doesn't mean that there aren't bad people. There are. There are some truly, truly shitty people out there.

And in here. Right in front of me.

That's when I figure it out.

No one is going to believe me.

No one is going to help because no one is going to listen, because Ander told his story first and he told it better.

No one is going to save me or screw him over.

I get it. That's the important part. I understand, so I can go forward.

"I was really drunk that night," I hear myself say.

He's still grinning. "Yeah," he says, and his voice is like it used to be when he talks to me: patient, teasing, playful, like I'm made of bird bones except when he's on top of me. "You really are a lightweight."

"I guess I am."

"So we're good?"

He almost looks sweet as he pushes himself upright, wincing. Almost hopeful.

"Yeah," I say. "Yeah, I guess we are."

Walk, I order myself. I walk to him and slide down

against the wall, slowly, next to him, leaving just enough space between our hands so that he knows I'm hesitant but here. Staying.

There is just one thing. "The notes," I say.

He laughs. No, but really. He actually fucking laughs. "Yeah," he says, awkward, aiming for adorable, bashful. "Sorry. I was—you know, frustrated. I missed you. Wes and I were talking, he told the guys . . . it got out of control. I'll talk to them. Don't worry."

Don't worry. Wouldn't that be so easy? Wouldn't that be so much nicer?

His fingers find mine.

His hands begin to roam.

"Are we still going to the dance?" he murmurs, leaning in. His breath is hot against my neck, and I really can smell him now. Everywhere.

"I can't," I say, and clear my throat a few times to get my voice back to normal. "I can't, my parents, it's just bad timing." Vague, vague. Lies don't have detail. "But they're leaving right after the dance." Dad's had this conference planned for months—he goes every year, and of course Mom will go with him this time. "Maybe you could come over?"

"Yes," he says, almost before I'm done asking.

"I was thinking of having a bonfire," I say. "Everyone

could come over after the dance tomorrow. It'll be fun."

"Oh," he says. "I thought it'd just be us."

His hand is roaming, roaming, roaming.

I make myself stay. I make myself talk. "Well, they'll have to leave eventually."

His face is against mine now and I can feel it when he laughs. "Sounds great," he says, his voice low, and then he's kissing me.

He turns so that I'm cornered against the floor and the wall and he's on top of me, my face in his hands, my lips in his mouth. I let him.

And when I finally break away, when he finally comes up for air and I can make excuses—parents, homework, I don't know what I say to get out of there, but I'm out of there. I smile and promise and apologize, and then I run like Cinderella from Prince Charming with Ander's wallet tucked into the front of my jeans.

Life is messy and the universe has an awful lot of people to keep track of. Sometimes things get screwed up. Sometimes bad things happen to good people. Sometimes good things happen to bad people.

That isn't fair.

Bad things should happen to bad people.

And they will. They will.

after

Friday morning, Dewey comes over with pot brownies and shit wine. At that point, I would have chugged piss if it would get my head to stop pounding. It's easier to get blind drunk and forget everything all over again.

We play Metatron: Sands of Time for a while. We eat a brownie each and Dewey decides that we're going to walk to the quarry when I tell him that I don't remember the last time I went outside. We pour the wine into a water bottle and put on our coats.

"I miss her," I say as we trudge along the road. The wind makes our teeth chatter.

"No shit," says Dewey. He throws back the wine and stumbles onto the shoulder. The rocks are slippery and he comes up choking. "God. This really is horrible. Here."

I tilt the bottle and swish it in my mouth. It is too sharp

and not strong enough, sweet enough to numb my mouth but not my head.

"No," I say, "but I don't usually. Usually I know she's dead, but not dead enough for me to actually miss her, you know?"

"Not really," he says, grabbing the bottle. I protest, and he just switches hands so the bottle's out of reach. "Dude, you're on the brink of losing your shit again, and I need to be drunk to deal with it." He waves a hand for me to continue. "You were spilling your heart or something?"

"Fuck off, dude."

"Touchy."

"I didn't ever think it'd feel like this," I say. My breath hangs in the air, and there are brief pockets of warmth where I walk through the words. "Her dying, I mean. I always figured that I'd die before her. I figured we'd all die before her. Like, she would have been the only one at our hundred-year reunion or whatever."

"Don't be a shithead. No one's going to be at our hundred-year reunion. Hell, no one's coming back for the five-year reunion."

That was probably true.

"Look, dude," Dewey says when the quarry comes into view. "You just gotta, you know. Live like she's still here or whatever."

I laugh. "I didn't live while she was here. I played Metatron and got drunk with you on Friday nights."

"And you're very fucking welcome," he says, and passes me the bottle again. We get to the quarry and keep walking along the edge. The sun hurts my eyes, and so does the ice, and Janie is still absent. I imagine her, though. If everything had gone right, we might be here anyway, tonight. She might have climbed through my window, and we might have driven to the quarry with stolen ice skates.

It's a nice thought, and god knows that there aren't enough of those in the world. So I drink, and I think about that.

"Dude," Dewey says later, slurring. We've almost made it around the quarry. "You're hogging the shit wine."

"Am not," I say. I'm slurring too.

It takes him two tries to snatch the bottle away. He throws it back, and eventually he lowers the bottle, but his head is still raised. "Hey, look. Look at that sun. Asshole."

I lie back too. The grass is freezing, and the sun is huge. "Is there anything you don't have a problem with?"

He thinks about it for a while. "Nah," he says.

"Janie loved the stars," I tell him. But she never meant it. Or maybe she did, I don't know. If she loved them, if she loved anything, it was because it burned.

I take another sip of wine, but I tilt it too sharply and it fills my nose and collar. Everything burns. I have swallowed a star.

And I said to the star, consume me.

Did she say that once? I think she did. It was probably Virginia Woolf who said it first.

I take another drink, because it doesn't matter what the hell Janie Vivian was or wasn't, because she's dead.

The sun is so bright.

"Did they find her body?" I ask him later. "Do they know what happened? Was she just so drunk she walked into the quarry?"

Dewey is quiet for a while before he asks, "You sure you want to know?"

"What do you mean?" The words feel slow, deliberate. I am learning to talk. I am remembering the existence of certain words.

"I mean," Dewey says, "I mean—nothing. Never mind."

"What? I fucking hate when you do that."

"Just leave it alone, Micah," he says. "Just let her be dead. You'll probably forget right after I tell you anyway, so it doesn't even matter."

He reaches for the bottle, and I hand it to him. "Fuck," he says. Oh, right. Empty. "You asshole," he says, and then he throws the bottle over the edge. "Look, Micah. The night of the bonfire, you—I mean, we—"

"You punched me," I say. "You broke my head open."

He goes quiet. He clears his throat. "Look, Micah, you're a suspect because you were with her. You guys were alone, which was fucking stupid of both of you, because no one knows that you're on, like, speaking terms. No one knows what you were doing. Are you listening? Dude."

I want to look over the edge. I want to see if it was the bottle that shattered or the ice, or the world. Or my head. It might be my head, honestly. But the world is tilting or spinning or falling or all three

and suddenly the air is colder and stuck in my chest and—

But then Dewey's hand is on my collar and choking me back, and I grin at him and say, "Hey. Thanks. You just saved my life. Again."

He's gasping and telling me to fuck myself, and he's so close and Janie's back again, finally back, her voice in my ear and her breath tickling my neck, whispering.

"I keep trying to tell you," she says. "I *told* you he was in love with you."

Dewey's eyes are blue. Very, very blue.

And then I'm kissing him, and all I can think is that I

must be very, very drunk, and that he tastes like cigarettes and shitty wine.

On the night of the bonfire, I was walking to my car, and Dewey caught my arm. I wobbled and almost fell, and then shook him off.

"What the hell, man? Are you following me?"

Dewey doesn't pull his cigarette out to answer. "Jesus, Micah. How much have you had? Do you not remember texting me? Give me the keys."

He tries to reach into my pocket, and I almost swing at him.

I remember the cold and the dark, and the way Dewey was lit by the tip of his cigarette. I remember this, the anger; the pounding, pressing fury at the spot where my brain stem met my spine.

But not why.

"Dammit, Micah, just get in the car. I want to go to bed."

His hand is on my arm again and I think about what Janie said, how Dewey was in love with me the way I was in love with her, and how shitty that was. How shitty it all was.

"Get off me," I snap. "Stop hitting on me, Dewey. I'm not fucking interested."

He is frozen. His hand is still on my arm, but it's starting to hurt.

"What did you say?"

"I said, stop fucking hitting on me—"

Then he punched me.

My head breaks open. It fucking bursts.

"Fuck you," he spits. His eyes are eclipsed. "Just—*fuck* you, Micah."

I squint, and the universe lurches before it focuses on his face.

"She said you were in love with me," I mumble. The fire is too hot. The lights are too bright. The world is melting.

"She's a goddamn fucking bitch, Micah!"

I am cracking. I am already falling apart.

"She's psychotic, she can't stand the idea of sharing you, and you just keep going back to her. You always go back. Why do you think she pulls you away every time I ask you to hang out? God, Micah. Just because—god, like I could see you panting after her and love you, like I could see the fucking toxic way you treat each other and—fuck it. Fuck you."

It's the last thing I remember. I wake up in the hospital.

The sun is huge and everywhere and burning my eyes out of their sockets.

"Oh, hell no. *No.* We're not doing this shit again."

But we do. Dewey pushes me, I fall, and this time, he lets me because he's already leaving. Gone. My head hits the ground and the sun explodes, and I know what will happen next. Or maybe what already happened.

The fire and the girl. I know what happened.

The Journal Of Janie Vivian

Once upon a time, a little girl cried Woolf.

Down in the village, people heard, but no one went to help.

"The wolves around here are nice wolves," said one of the villagers. "They wouldn't hurt a soul."

"She just wants attention," said another. "There probably isn't a wolf at all."

"Maybe she was wearing a red hood," offered another. "Red attracts wolves. Everyone knows that. If she was wearing red, she was just asking for it."

"She was probably flirting with the wolf," yelled another from the back. "She flirts with all the wolves!"

And so the villagers ignored her and went on with their lives.

From then on, the little girl held her breath and her tongue. She carried matches *in her pockets, so that if the villagers didn't come the next time she cried wolf, maybe they'd show up for the fire.*

FEAR NO MORE

before

"I don't get it," Micah says again. "What is all of this stuff? I thought we were going to your house. The bonfire?"

"Just chill," I tell him for the thousandth time. "All will be revealed in time. Just drive."

"Fine," he says. He's annoyed, he always seems to be annoyed now, we both do. It's inevitable, considering the amount of time I'm spending in his house, which is ironic since we both thought the problem was that I moved away, but whatever. Tonight is our new beginning. We're starting over.

Purification.

The silence is humid between us, but he drives toward the Metaphor without me telling him to, and I know it's all going to be okay. I know it will be because it has to be.

I get out of the car—his, and he didn't even argue when I got in the driver's seat, just looked at me like I was going to snap, so I guess that shows how well I'm holding together—and pop the trunk, and he follows me, then stops. I don't look at him, but I know he's blinking, rapidly, and each time he closes and opens his eyes, his eyebrows draw a little lower until they're almost at his nose.

We usually take Micah's car on ninja missions because of the trunk. You can say a lot of things about Micah's car, but the trunk could hold a body.

He doesn't ask.

But he leans into the trunk and grabs a box. The trunk is filled with boxes, most of them open. I got them from my garage earlier—it's all the stuff I never unpacked because I couldn't stand being in that fucking house. But there's also a big one, an old UPS box I'd scrounged from the recycling bin at school, and it's filling most of the trunk. That's the one Micah takes. He has his feet planted and shoulders square, but it's a lot lighter than he thinks. He flies back with the box, and I almost laugh. This is better. This is Micah, just a little bit off-balance and always embarrassed. My Micah.

Me and you, I think as I walk toward what's left of the Metaphor. It doesn't matter. It won't after tonight. *You and me.*

That's all that matters, in the end.

We carry boxes back and forth, stacking them higher and higher beside the Metaphor. Once they're all there, we start ripping them apart and pulling out the papers: notes Ander and I passed back and forth, from seventh grade all the way to this year. The rest of the fairy tale bullshit and all of the books. And other stuff too, stuff I just don't want anymore. Old notebooks and loose papers, binders of bio notes with margins full of doodles and Skarpie bleeding through.

"God, I'm an actual hoarder," I say, dumping a box of coloring books onto the ground.

"Janie," Micah says.

He's on his knees, digging through the mess. I think about stopping him, but he should know. No more secrets between us, no more lies.

"Janie," he says again, and his face is slack with disbelief. "These are your journals."

I roll my eyes. "I know. I put them in your car, Micah. *Duh.*"

"But these . . . Janie, these are your *journals.*"

He flips through Journal Ten, which was back when I was still in my sketchbook journal phase. I see the ink, watercolor, so many sketches. I did a drawing a day for months and months. There must be a hundred Metaphors in there.

"You can't do this," he says. He shoves his hands into his armpits to keep warm, and I step closer and tug them out and press them between mine. Not that my hands are warm either, but at least now we're shivering together.

"You can't, all of your plans are in here. You want to do all of that shit, draw and go to Nepal and write about it in your journals and—"

"I'm not burning Journal Twelve." Yet. And I'm not going to Nepal, either. I never was. Micah was right—I would have wished and wanted but I would have been too scared to do anything. Just like everybody else. Everyone says they want to travel and leave home and find themselves or whatever, but they never do it. That's what high school's for. You make plans and you don't follow through. You dream and you can be brave when you're dreaming, brave enough to imagine that there's actually a *yourself* to find, brave enough to finish projects even though you were never born with endings, brave enough to plan volunteer trips even though you'd probably be dead of asphyxiation by the time you're there because you're always holding your breath as if that can keep you together. Please. I'm in so many pieces that there's nothing left to hold. The plane ticket doesn't change that. I'm still terrified. Maybe Micah can get a refund.

"But the rest of these. What was the point? You always wanted to look at them later. You wanted to look back through them one day, you wanted to remember all of the shit we did, that we're going to do. You wrote it all down, you can't just get rid of it, or what's the point?"

"Oh, Micah." My hands are clenched tight around his. Our hands are actually sweating now, or it might just be mine. "There was never a point. Don't you see?"

I drop his hands, reach into my pocket, light a match.

I drop the match and watch as it falls from my fingers.

Watch as the starving flame yearns back toward my fingertips just a little as it falls.

And falls.

All that paper sure burns awfully fast.

It burns and burns and burns.

I watch for a while before I open the last box. The big one. No, that's not true. I don't open it, I tear it apart. I use fingers and feet and teeth and I destroy it, rip the sides out and throw them into the water. The fire is at my back and spreading into my bloodstream—I am furious. I am rabid.

When it's sufficiently mauled, I step back.

Behind me, Micah inhales—a sharp sound that I swear makes the fire lean toward him.

"What?" I say. "I had to. I couldn't get them into the box."

His hands are up, eyes wide. "Janie. Janie, stop. You can't do this."

"Watch me," I say. He reaches for my shoulders to hold

me back, and I flinch away, and snarl, "Get the fuck off me, Micah."

His hands drop away like I have turned to fire. I wish, but alas.

"But you were going to finish them," he says. His eyes are too big for his head. "Janie, they—they're beautiful. Just . . . come on, Janie. Don't do this. You can finish them, I know you can."

"Art isn't finished," I tell him. "It's abandoned. Who said that?"

"Da Vinci," he says, so quietly I almost don't hear.

"Exactly. And if it's going to be abandoned, it might as well burn."

And I hand him the match.

His face goes white. "What? No."

"Just do it. I can't do it, so you have to. You have to. For me."

"Janie, you don't know what you're saying—"

"I do know. Why is that so hard to believe? I know. I know what I want and what I want is for you to take this match and light it and drop it. Okay? Micah. Please. I love you more than anything. Please just do it."

He's biting the inside of his cheek so hard that he must be bleeding. He can't hold himself back from asking. "But why?"

I don't look at him. "Stop it. You don't want to know why."

Out of the corner of my eye, I see him *almost*. Almost ask why again. Almost press the issue. Almost change my mind. But he doesn't. He leaves it at that.

And he lights the match.

And he drops it.

"Everything."

They burn quickly, feathers first, curling black. Then the bamboo. It only takes a minute or so until there's nothing to save.

Purification. You burn everything, you burn and burn and burn, and you start over. This fire isn't quite big enough for that. This fire is just for me, for everything Janie Vivian ever was. I stare for a little longer and then I go to the barn for vodka and buckets. When I come back out, Micah's eyes are on me, wary and uncertain, but waiting all the same.

"I think most people are embers," I say.

He takes a deep breath, and doesn't answer for a long time. When he does, finally, it's just to say, "Okay."

"Embers. Most people are just waiting for a breath to coax them to life. Some of the lucky ones are the breath. But some people aren't either."

I hand Micah a bottle of vodka, and he starts drinking right away. I wait for him to take at least what I estimate to be six shots before I fill the buckets in the quarry. The fire screams as I put it out, and it makes me want to cry.

I don't, though. I take Micah's hand and lead him to the car. I drive us to my house, where people are already arriving.

after

DECEMBER 19

When everything comes back into focus, it is nearly dark. The moon is huge and rising. I am freezing. I can't feel my fingertips.

I remember and then I don't.

I forget and then it all comes rushing back.

I lose count of how many times I throw up.

I lose track of when I stop counting.

I don't know how I got there but I am lying in the grass. Then I am lying on the rocks. Then the grass. The world is vertical and horizontal and nothing but sky. I don't know what's happening but it might be that nothing is happening at all.

"Janie," I whisper. The stars are cold and burning, like her. The stars are unreachable and everything, like her. "Janie, Janie."

"Micah? Is that you?"

~

Janie was driving. It was my car, but Janie was driving. Her hair was wild; the windows were rolled down even though it was cold already. It would snow soon. I remember thinking about that as I took another shot.

"All right!" Janie screamed. I jumped. The bottle was already at my lips and I gulped down more cheap vodka than I could handle, and I could handle a lot. I coughed, almost choked, almost puked.

Janie's head was half out of the window and she was driving too fast. Her hair streamed behind her, brighter than her wings on fire.

Her wings on fire. I had set her wings on fire.

"You and me," she screamed as the car swerved back and forth and I tried to keep the vodka in the bottle. "You and me, universe! Let's fucking go!"

I remember the relief. She was insane, and this was Janie. This was the Janie who loved fire and carried rocks. This was the Janie Vivian who trusted rarely but deeply, and hoped with everything she was. This was the Janie Vivian, who I had loved with every atom in every cell in my body before memory was relevant.

Maybe she heard me think that. Maybe she had always been right about our souls being joined, because she came back into the car and ran a finger down my arm, shoulder to elbow, feather light, and down to my knuckles. She stopped when our fingertips met and kept them there until we pulled into her driveway. We had to park at the bottom because it was already clogged with cars.

It wasn't until she moved away to pull the keys out of the ignition that I realized that she had been shaking.

"I'm glad you're here," she said, voice barely audible. The lights in the car were dimming, and she was going dark.

"We can fix this," I said. My tongue was thick. "You and me."

We can do anything, she always said. *Anything, everything. You and me against the world.*

"Don't," she said. There was a flash of light as she lit a match and blew it out. "Don't do that. Don't pretend. That's my thing. You're supposed to be the one person who never pretends. So why are you pretending?"

I didn't have an answer to that. Most of the time, I didn't know how to respond to her. Most of the time, I didn't need to.

She just shook her head a little and raised the bottle back to my lips. "Drink."

"Why?" I asked.

"Because the universe doesn't give a shit, Micah," she said. "So why should we?"

~

It takes my eyes a while to focus. I know it isn't Janie. I know but I still hope, even though her eyes are too dark and her hair is too short and her face is too sharp. Even though she is in running clothes, and Janie does not believe in running. Even though she is crying, and Janie refuses to cry anymore.

"God," she says. Her voice is thick with tears and I want her to leave. I want to lie here and squint at the moon until the sky becomes white. "God, I wish I hadn't, okay? Okay? Stop following me around. Stop looking at me like that. I know she told you, I know she did. I tried to tell her—I tried to apologize but—"

"Piper?" I ask, because I'm not sure. "Piper?"

She's on the ground next to me now, crouching with her head in her arms. Arms on her knees. She gasps out muffled sobs.

"I was drunk too." I think this is what she says. "I was drunk, I just wanted to go home. I didn't mean to—I didn't mean for him to . . ."

Home. Home would be a nice place to be. I wish I could get there. Or remember where it is. Or where I am.

"I left her," Piper whispers, not that anyone is listening. "I let her go."

No, I'm at the Metaphor. I know that. It is December, not September. It is cold, and it will snow soon. Janie moved away on the last day of summer vacation before senior year, which was months ago, and I am still trying to remember. She made wings, and burned them. I burned them. She declared an apocalypse, but it had already started. She believed and stopped believing in love. None of it matters, because she is dead. She fell into the quarry and never quite came out. And on the night she fell into the quarry and never came out, she had a bonfire.

"I didn't—I didn't mean to," she says. "I didn't know what to do, what was I supposed to do? I couldn't—I didn't know—oh god, I didn't mean for it to happen, I didn't. I didn't. Oh god. She asked me to stay."

At that bonfire, I was on the ground.

Gravel on my palms. Puke in my throat.

Janie's dragging me up. She sighs. "Dammit. I forgot how unsteady you get. I wish I could take a shot. I love being drunk. Did you know that? Of course you do. I love it, Micah. I love not giving a shit. God, you're so tall. I hate that."

"Take a shot," I say, thrusting the bottle at her. She steadies me.

"Not tonight," she says.

We walk for forever. "Why is your driveway so long?"

She almost laughs. "I had to park far away. Everyone's

going to clog the driveway later and I don't want to get stuck. We have to get out of here fast. Oh, wait. Here." She slips my keys back into my pocket. Her fingers are cold.

"Why?"

"Why what?"

"Why do we have to get out of here fast?"

She doesn't answer. I don't ask again.

The house finally comes into view. She drags me into the backyard and over to a lawn chair and goes to light the fire. There are marshmallows on a long table, and other shit, but I only care about the marshmallows. I don't think I can get to them. I take another swallow of vodka instead.

Soon there are other kids from school too, everyone from school and maybe I talk to them and maybe I don't. There are chairs all around, and blankets, and booze. I see the booze. It's almost like Janie cleaned out her parents' cabinets and put it all on the table.

And eventually I see the fire.

It is at the very back of the yard and the house is behind us. More cars are coming, cars spilling out the senior class of Waldo High. Janie really did invite everyone. They whoop and punch each other, and eventually this turns into chasing each other, and eventually this turns to chasing each other with torches.

For a while, Janie walks around, talks to people. She

smiles. Her eyes are pale, and I watch the fire reflected in them. I start playing a drinking game with myself. Sip every time she laughs and touches someone's arm. Sip every time she flips her hair over her shoulder. Shot every time she looks back at me.

Finally she comes back. I don't remember seeing that. One moment she wasn't there and the next she was, dark and backlit against the fire. There was a blanket in her arms. She climbed into my lap and threw it over us. We sat and did not speak, but we listened.

It was not warm or cold.

It was not dark or bright.

It just was.

Here, it is quiet except for Piper's sniffles. I wish she would stop.

"Are you staying?" I ask her, because I want to leave.

Her head snaps up. Her jaw is slack and her eyes are drowning, drowning.

She slaps me. My head snaps back. When it comes back down, Piper is leaving too.

And I am drowning, drowning.

No, wait.

That's not right.

Not quite.

The Journal Of Janie Vivian

*Once upon a time, Sleeping Beauty is raped
and only wakes up when she gives birth to
twins.*

Once upon a time, the little mermaid dies.

*Once upon a time, true love's kiss doesn't
work on Snow White, but the prince carts
the corpse back to the castle anyway.*

*Once upon a time Scheherazade tells sto-
ries to stay alive. Rapunzel carts her chil-
dren around a desert and almost starves.
The miller's daughter is too afraid to say no.
Little Red Riding Hood loses her virginity.
Janie Vivian tries to remember to breathe.*

The end.

before

The hard part is over. Phase three was the crucial one, everything from buying gas with Ander's Visa to throwing the card back into his car when I went to hug him hello. I was careful: no one saw me, no one looked twice, I didn't leave fingerprints.

Oh, right, I forgot to mention: I have a new plan. A new ninja mission. This one is four phases. Arson is easier than love.

Phase four is the fun part. It's also the pot in my yard and the shitty music and the couples probably having sex in our lawn chairs even though it's so cold that we'll probably hear about someone having frostbite on his dick tomorrow, but I just have to wait that out. People just need to get a little more drunk.

Micah's sprawled in a lawn chair and I'm against him, so that he's leaning back as far as he can and my head is on his arm and I'm fetal on his chest. He weaves in and out of consciousness and stares at the house. Even in the dark it's ugly and stupid and obscene. But soon that won't be a problem anymore, so I try not to think about it.

His eyelashes flutter. He shakes his head, or tries to, and looks around.

"This is kind of lame," he says, and I only understand because I know him so well. His words are garbled and adorable.

"Yup," I say. "But the fun part is coming." *Just you wait.*

His head is drooping, and my heart does a funny thudding thing. Maybe I made him drink too much. I tap his cheek. "Micah? Hello? Look at me."

He tries, and I know I probably shouldn't, but I giggle. He's so confused and sweet, and he's trying. He really is.

"Tell me a secret. No, don't. I don't want to tell secrets tonight." We have enough secrets as it is. We have too many. "Tell me about your favorite day."

"Huh?"

"Your favorite day. Us, together. Your favorite day."

He tries to scratch his head. He blinks up at me, trying to focus.

"What are you thinking?" he asks me.

I almost laugh. What am I thinking? What am I not thinking?

I am thinking about Ander and the kind of love that starts and ends with lips. I am thinking about Piper and me curled in a bus seat with the same music thrumming in our brains and our zero-accountability friendship and how I would have stayed with her no matter what. I am thinking about the little girls in Nepal and how there is probably no Micah in their lives. Micah. Most of all, I'm thinking about him. I am thinking of his face in the window across from mine. I am thinking about the conversations neither of us remember. I am thinking about the times I wanted to say thank you but couldn't find the words and the times I wanted to say I'm sorry but couldn't find the guts. I am thinking of his face when I kissed Ander at regionals. I am thinking of the way I used him. I am thinking of the way his face tenses when he's annoyed and the way the same face dimples when he smiles.

I am thinking about the way we love each other. I am thinking about our soul, one atom and bruised all over now that I have dragged it behind me with my muddy hands.

"Micah?" I say.

"Yeah?"

"Do you think there are things that can't be fixed?"

He shifts against me. I watch the fire, and even though

I know him down to his fingertips, I don't know what he will say next.

"What do you mean?"

He tries to push me away, but I can't, *I can't let go.*

"Do you mean—do you mean us?"

"No," I say. I wrap my fingers in his shirt and pull him close. "Never us. Never."

"Okay," he says, like *thank god*, and I hide my smile against his shoulder. "I dunno, Janie. I don't know what you're talking about."

I sigh. I grab the bottle, take a quick shot myself, just one, and squeeze my eyes closed as I swallow. "Okay," I say, "how about this. If you could go back in time and redo one thing, what would it be?"

I catch him off guard. He blinks. His head falls back, and I touch his throat where it quivers with an answer he doesn't quite want to give.

"I wouldn't have gone with my babysitter," he says, so quietly I barely catch it. "I would have made my dad stay."

"But your mom would still be dead." He flinches. "Wait, sorry. Sorry," I say again, quieter. I lay my head against his chest and listen to his heart beating, beating, beating. "I just—don't you see? Everything would still have happened as it happened."

"Yeah," he says. "I guess."

those maybes. All of those could haves, would

"I've been thinking about that a lot lately." I can't stop, I can't stop replaying all of the ways this could have gone right, if we had just tried a little harder. If we had made smaller mistakes. "Whatever you do, whatever you redo, it all ends up here. Some things are just unavoidable. No matter how hard you try, the things meant to go to shit still go to shit. Terrible things happen, Micah, and you can't stop them. You just can't."

So you just do more terrible things.

"Oh," he says, frowning. He's bleary and blinking and trying to focus on me, and my love for him is sudden and sharp and everything. I kiss him on the nose.

"Favorite day," I say again. "Story time. I want to hear about your favorite day."

"Uh. Um. The fish? You remember the fish?"

And he stops there. My eyes fly open and I glare at him. "That wasn't a story. I wanted a story."

"Jesus, Janie, grow up." But he complies. "The night we put fish in Grant Ebber's car and he didn't find it for a week?"

"Tell me about the night," I mumble. I could fall asleep here. The music is too loud and the smoke is giving me a headache, but it's not so hard to pretend again, pretend that it's just us, behind the smoke screen and impenetrable music.

But then, it's never hard to pretend.

"God, Janie, I don't remember the night. It was raining? Not at first, it was just cloudy, and I was already in bed, and you were—you were so angry."

"Of course I was angry," I say. "The shit they were saying about Myra—it was just. Ugh. People, Micah. People are the worst."

He presses on. He's starting to slur. "Right, he dumped her because he said she was blowing the basketball team for luck. Not that that worked. And people said her breath smelled fishy and you just wanted to prove that it wasn't true. So we went to Pick 'n Save and bought the two biggest fish we could find. And we put them in his trunk, and then we went back to my house and climbed onto the roof and picked superpowers in the rain."

I slide down a bit, rearrange myself so that my head is in the crook of his elbow, and look up at him. I remembered that night too, the heavy, heavy rain on the roof of the car, the cashier with the pink ombre hair who laughed and told us we were crazy kids and told Micah not to let me go. I remember dancing when we got back, waltzing in the driveway and stepping on his feet and him stepping on mine, tripping and stumbling and soaked through, and laughing with our heads thrown back, drinking the rain like we were dying of thirst.

"But why that day?" I ask. "Why that one?"

"I don't know," he says, and sighs. "I guess. I guess because you were, you know. Insane. Completely crazy. You didn't care if we were caught, you know? You didn't care so much that I didn't care either. We were in the rain and you were warm, and you smelled like cinnamon and vodka and lemons and sleep and, I don't know, something sharper—why are you smiling all weird?"

"Oh, Micah," I say, "you big sap."

I didn't think he noticed things like that.

"Okay, my turn," I say, scooting closer. "My favorite day ever was the time we went to the petting zoo freshman year. I sat next to the cute German exchange student on the bus. Remember him? Hans? He got sent back after a few months because he got caught with pot too many times? We took a trip to the petting zoo and the farm for bio, and you and I got partnered up, and we ran off to the edge of the orchard while everyone else dissected apples, and we climbed into this one tree and ate all the apples we could and everything tasted like sunshine. There was this old barn, they were halfway through tearing it down, and I wanted to explore it, but you said we couldn't, we had to get back. So we did, and everyone was at the petting zoo part, feeding lambs and stuff. And Mr. Marvin was talking to the farmer, and we overheard them saying that the tagged ones, the tagged animals were going to become lamb steaks and veal, and it was so shitty, Micah. I wanted to cry. I think I did cry. So we went back that night. We slid under the fence with masks and picket signs and a thermos of hot chocolate and graham crackers and marshmallows, and we stood under the single security camera and protested. You remember? The signs were kind of lame—"

"You made them!"

"Like, SAVE THE ANIMALS and WE WILL NOT BE CAGED and stuff like that. And after, after we did our part for the planet or the cause or whatever, we went to the old barn, and you said there would be rats and snakes and crap, but we went anyway, and we opened the thermos and it was hot chocolate and we dumped the marshmallows in and dunked the graham crackers and watched the stars chase the moon across the sky."

Micah just watches me. He flicks my hair. "You're lying," he says. "Your eyebrow is doing the . . . the thing."

"The thing?" I say, and he affirms, "The thing," and I laugh because he's right.

"I'm lying," I say, and then I hook my foot around his scrawny hips and pull myself upright so that we're face to face. My hands are on his chest and I can feel his heart, thudding thudding thudding. "I'm lying," I say again, "you're right. My favorite day, my favorite favorite day ever, is this one."

And I kiss him.

It's soft and hesitant and yielding.

He doesn't move and I still don't quite breathe.

And then—

And then—

He leans, I push. He is rainwater and smoke and wishes. He is honey and wind and bitter as truth and sharp with hurting and endlessly, unbearably sweet. He is air, finally, endlessly. Ease—that's what it is, that's what we are, we snap into place, or we glide, or we fall. His fingers are careful, light, resting on my back and my waist, barely touching. My hands are over his lungs and his heart, pressing. He is Micah and I am Janie, and this is how we should have done it years and years ago.

We kiss like that for a long time. Centuries, maybe. Eons.

But then there's a whistle. Not a nice one. It's sharp and rising and it pierces the music and slices into my eardrums, and I let go of Micah and look up, and it's Ander and Piper, and he's grinning the ugliest grin in the world, and she just looks like she wants to get out of here.

Again.

And suddenly I'm cold. I am carved out of ice.

"Jeez, Janie," Ander says. He leans his elbows on the back of the lawn chair with his cup crooked in his hand, dribbling onto us. "Micah Carter? Seriously, who won't you fuck?"

But I'm looking at Piper. Staring her down, even if she won't look at me.

The fury is sudden and harsh and rising. It's impulse. I look straight at Piper and I spit out, "Wait. *Stay.*"

Ander grins, and kisses me.

I am too surprised to stop him.

I am too slow to say no.

And Piper.

Piper finally looks at me, and she doesn't stop him.

He pulls me out of the chair with his stupid, stupid wrestler body as he keeps kissing me, and the blanket falls off and the cold hits me everywhere and all at once, and his stubble stabs my face and his breath is stale booze, and I wish he were grosser so that I could puke in his mouth.

And he obliges. He reaches for the bottom of my shirt and I'm not frozen, I'm drowning in liquid nitrogen, I'm frostbitten, I'm cryogenic.

But I still feel it when something shifts behind me, and all of a sudden, I don't care about Piper or Ander. But by the time I push Ander away, by the time I can breathe enough to get away from them, Micah is disappearing into the dark.

"Micah," I try, but my voice is stuck somewhere deep inside me, rotting away with all of the stomach butterflies that had reanimated for a few seconds when Micah and I touched. But they're good and safely dead again, and clogging my throat.

"Don't worry about him," Ander says. "Come on, Janie. Let's stop fucking around." And his hand is on my wrist, and I whirl around and shout it at him.

"No!"

And I punch him across the face, just in case the message wasn't clear.

Piper's watching me, horrified, mouth open and useless and stupid.

"Fuck you," I say, and I mean it, I really do, I don't hate anyone like I hate her right then.

And then I'm pushing past them, running. The blanket falls off and the air is so cold it hurts, everywhere. "Micah," I scream, and I'm crying. "Micah, wait."

He's halfway down the driveway already, though, and he hesitates for maybe a second before he turns around again, but the second is enough. The moment. The moment has to be enough.

"Micah," I say, and I run into him, crash, collide. His

breath whooshes out of him and mine disappears. Or it was never there in the first place. "Micah, don't leave, just listen, listen to me—"

"I'm tired," he says, very, very quietly, and I hiccup into silence. He's looking at the ground, playing with his car keys in sloppy fingers.

"Micah, stop, you can't drive like this, just stop—"

"I'm not driving. I'm finding Dewey. He's driving."

The anger that rises in me isn't rational, I know, but I can't help spitting out, "Of course he is. And where is he? God, Micah, you keep going to him because he's in love with you, but don't you see? It doesn't matter. He isn't here. Here is *us*, Micah. You and me. Me and— "

He turns away. "I'm tired," he says again, far, far away. "Janie, I'm just really fucking sick of this, okay?"

"Of what?"

And that's when he looks up. Snaps up. His eyes meet mine and I realize that this isn't what I want, I don't want to look at him, not at all, not like this. He is so far gone that I don't know—I don't know if he will come back.

"I am sick," he says slowly, deliberately, spitting the words out syllable by syllable. "I am sick of being screwed over by you. Every single time. I'm tired of you and all of your shit."

"My shit?" I say, my voice rising on every word, every

letter. "Yes, I have shit, Micah, you know why? Because I was fucking ra—"

Throat clogged, need plunger. I can't get the word out. I choke on it. I swallow it back down.

Micah laughs. He rubs his face with the heel of his hand and tries to shake the vodka from his head and pushes me out of the way. "What's that, Janie? What aren't you telling me this time?" He shakes his head. "Someone fucked you over, huh? How does it feel?"

And he's walking down the driveway, and I can't think about what he said, I can't; but I also can't let him go. "Micah," I say. "Micah, but *us*. But *you and me*."

For ever.

For everything.

Janie and Micah.

Micah and Janie.

"Micah," I scream. "Micah, more than anything. Do you hear me? *I love you more than anything.*"

He looks back. He looks straight into my eyes and says, "Don't. Get the hell away from me, Janie. I'm going home. Just . . . don't. We should just. We should stop trying, Janie."

And he does that. He walks away.

I watch him go, and I'm shaking so hard that the world is almost blurring. But I take a breath. I hold it. I pull myself together. Micah will come back, because he has to. For now, I have more important things to do. I have to make sure the universe stays in balance. That the wicked are punished, even if the good are rarely rewarded.

Let the fun begin.

The maximum sentence for rape is hard to find. I know. I looked. It's hard to find because it's hard to convict, which is funny. Imagine this: you are a victim. You are a victim, and the person who gave you that bruised label is probably never going to get punished because no one believes you, if you ever even get the chance to say anything at all. He will never go to jail and he'll never understand what it is to be trapped, to rot.

Rape? *Rape* is a word that no one wants to shout or hear. But let's say—

—let's just say—

That we let dead horses lie and rot and breed maggots. We never say that word out loud again. That's okay.

There are other crimes.

I've wanted to see my room for a while now. To see where it all started and ended, but what a shitty ending. I haven't gone yet. I didn't even go upstairs when I was setting up for the bonfire. I didn't even leave the kitchen. I only needed to pillage the garage for all the stuff to burn. I hadn't come back at all before today. I haven't even talked to my parents in ages, so I guess that means they don't want me back. It's kind of weird. They spent an awful lot of time tracking my whereabouts for eighteen years, and that all seems like kind of a waste now.

The gas is in the garage, and I go in through a side door. All the lights are off, and we're too far from the bonfire for anyone to see me, not that anyone would have missed me, anyway. It'll take minutes. Seconds. I lug the cans upstairs two by two. From the upstairs window, I can see the bonfire and the bright specks of the torches the guys wave around. I take a deep breath.

I push open the door to my room.

Oh god. Oh god—*how?* How can it possibly still smell like him?

I had this whole dramatic pouring ritual planned out—I was going to soak the bed and then go out in circles around it, but I just run in holding my breath and let loose. The gasoline spills out desperately. It waterfalls.

I do the rest quickly. The living room and the kitchen. The foyer and the den. I do Mom and Dad's room last. I imagine their faces as I pour, and smile. Their beautiful ugly house in ashes, their ugly beautiful daughter with a story they might finally, finally hear.

And then I go back to my room. I pull Journal Twelve and a match out of my coat pocket. Quick, quick movements, no thinking necessary. I light the match and lay it on the journal pages and drop the journal, and it happens.

I run.

My chest is still tight tight tight, but I'm running. Out the side door, back into the party, where people are still drinking and chasing each other. No one even sees me until I start screaming.

"Fire!"

after

"Micah? Micah, can you hear me? Stay on the line, Micah."

"Dewey."

"Yeah, man, it's me. Where are you? Why aren't you at home? Are you still at the quarry? Jesus. Have you been there all day?"

"Dewey, I saw you. After Janie. You were by the police cars."

"Okay, I'm going to call your dad—"

"I told her that I never wanted to see her again. That we should stop trying. Did you know that? I didn't want to, really. I was really drunk."

"Are you drunk now? How drunk are you?"

"You shouldn't have told me that she was a nutcase. I was still trying not to go back. I still loved her. I still do. But she was insane. She set the fire, you know."

"Okay, great, we can talk about that later—"

"But she kept trying to tell me that I only kept you around because you loved me. I was really sad, Dewey. I was really sad. I thought she might be right. I'm sorry. But she kept telling me."

"Yeah, well, I mean, fuck her, but—"

"I'm sorry I kissed you. I'm sorry. I'm sorry you had to watch me these past weeks too. That must have sucked. My dad wasn't really paying you, was he?"

"Micah, I need you to focus and tell me where the fuck you are, okay? Hey, just—"

"I figured he wasn't. You're an awesome guy, Dewey. Did you know that? You're awesome."

"Fuck it, I'll come get you. Stay where you are—"

"I've finally figured it out, Dewey. I think I finally figured out all—oh. Oh shit. Oh god."

"Micah—"

"Oh god, Dewey, oh god. Oh, god. It was me. I remember, I remember what I said to her. Dewey, oh fucking shit, *fucking shit.*"

"Micah, breathe—"

"Fuck fuck fuck fuck, oh god, oh my god, she didn't fall, Dewey, she didn't fall into the quarry, did she. Did she? Oh shit, oh shit, oh fucking shit—"

"Micah? *Micah!*"

But that is all I hear.

I stare and stare at the ice over the quarry and all I can
see is her hair

sinking

lower.

before

The fire burns and burns.

It's all very nice and all, but—

Where's Micah?

The police and the fire department come. People are screaming and running around, and if they're getting burned, it's because of the torches. Someone just fell down the hill and probably sprained an ankle. Some people keep getting their fingers trampled on because they're drunk enough to think that stop, drop, and roll is a good idea while the sober ones run away.

I'm sitting on the curb and they don't even notice, except to tell me to move aside. The house is almost gone.

I don't know how long I sit there, staring and staring down the street, waiting for him to come back.

~

It begins to rain.

The house is gone, and now the police are starting to dig around.

I take a deep breath and pull myself together long enough to get out of there.

I go to the barn first. I put my matches and stone and the ticket to Nepal with our alcohol behind the rusty tractor. I don't feel right taking it. Maybe Micah can use the refund to pay off that speeding ticket. And I want him to have the rock.

Fear no more.

But I'm terrified. I sit on the floor of the barn and take little gulps of air but don't let anything out. I need Micah. Micah was my alibi. Micah was going to be too drunk to remember I wasn't with him all night.

My phone keeps vibrating in my pocket and I finally take it out. There's five missed calls from probably the police and a few *holy shit this is crazy are you okay where are you sorry about the house* texts and one from Ander that's just a picture of his middle finger.

It's so ridiculous—so *Ander*—that I almost laugh before I realize.

His middle finger isn't at the bonfire. He sent it a while ago, probably right after I ran after Micah, and he's in a car and not at my house and definitely, definitely not setting it on fire.

Oh god. Oh god, oh god.

Fuck. *Fuck*.

It isn't fair.

It's not, it's not fair, he's going to walk away from this and I'm—I'm going to still be asphyxiating burning shaking paralyzed terrified terrified terrified. No. *No*. He's going to get away with it, isn't he, of course he is, of course of course of course. There's a scream in my throat and too much air blocking it. It isn't, it isn't fair. How—how can the universe really not give a shit? *How*?

I try to take a breath but where the hell can I even let it out now? My stupid fucking house is gone and so is Micah. *Micah*. Oh, god, Micah. I try again but I'm shaking and my lungs have collapsed because it doesn't fucking matter, the police are going to figure out that it wasn't Ander at all, and it just *isn't fucking fair* and I can't do it anymore, I can't, because what's the point? Micah is gone, Micah isn't going to defend me. Oh, god. *Micah*.

I stand up.

It's very dark.

I push open the doors of the barn, and keep walking. I go to what's left of the Metaphor. I sit down in the furious rain and pull handfuls of rocks into my lap. I uncap the Skarpie and begin to write on the impossibly smooth rocks.

Slut.

Whore.

Bitch.

Nice ass, though.

Asking for it.

Liar.

Liar.

Liar.

Roses are red, violets are blue. You're a piece of shit, a raging bitch too.

Janie Vivian is a bore, Janie Vivian is a whore, Janie Vivian has no friends, Janie Vivian needs to end.

Slut.

Slut.

Whore.

Slut.

Slut.

Bitch.

Someone fucked you over, huh?

How does that feel?

And when I'm done, when they're in my pockets and sleeves and hood, I stare at the water and think about absence.

That's the truth, I guess. We don't catch moments in the passing. We don't catch them at all. We just reach and scramble and wish for fairy godmothers and Prince Charmings. It's too bad none of it is real. It really is too bad.

My name is Janie Vivian, and I don't exist.

The water is cold and it is rising.

It is rising higher and higher and higher still.

The moment has passed.

The end.

after

I never learned to light matches right. Somehow, I always burn my fingertips. I can never

actually

do it

right.

Or anything else, really.

I'm sorry, I don't have the guts to do it like you did. I can't walk it. But maybe I can just fall.

I drop the matches onto the ice, one by one. The ice is thin and dark. Behind me is the empty space where the Metaphor used to be. Where we spent every Thursday. Where we ate fries and counted stones and climbed and fell. Where you declared an apocalypse and I chose the music.

I watch the matches fall, and I think I can do that. I don't have to do anything, really. Just let the ice melt and break apart. Just let gravity do what gravity does. I can't screw that up. I've already screwed everything else up. I think I've figured it out. I think she wanted Ander to go to jail, and I want him to go to jail too, but I've fucked it all up.

I'm running out of matches. Ten or so left. I think about apocalypses.

Ten.

In 634 BCE, the Romans thought their city would disappear because it was the one hundred twentieth year of their founding, because Romulus had supposedly received twelve eagles from the gods when he discovered Rome, and the old, gray philosophers thought that each eagle represented a decade. But it passed, and the world didn't end, but the Romans still died eventually.

Nine.

Pope Sylvester II tells everyone that the world will end in 1000 CE, presumably because it's a nice even number. People freak out. Riots pop up all over Europe. People travel to Jerusalem to—to what? I don't know. The world doesn't end. They move on.

Eight.

Pope Innocent III, Islamophobe extraordinaire, tells everyone that the world will end six hundred and sixty years after the rise of Islam. He is wrong.

Seven.

The Black Plague hits Europe in 1346. People say it's a sign of the end of times, and for a lot of them, it is. Some of them die. Some of them don't. The world continues, but people stop throwing their shit on the streets.

Six.

Thomas Müntzer calls it the beginning of the apocalypse. Everyone else calls it 1525. He and his followers are killed by the government for some hazy reason that Wikipedia did not list and so was not included in my thesis paper. He himself dies under torture, *and* gets beheaded, so it was pretty apocalyptic for him.

Five.

Christopher Columbus jumps on the apocalypse-predicting bandwagon in 1501 and writes the *Book of Prophecies*, in which he says the world is going to end in 1656, after he is safely dead so he won't be around to witness it.

Four.

1666, just because it has the number six hundred and sixty-six in it. Just because.

Three.

1806. Some chick named Mary Bateman has a hen that lays an egg that proclaims the second coming of Christ. Rich people worship the chicken. Poor people starve because they don't have chicken. Turns out that Mary

Bateman went to a lot of trouble to etch the words onto the egg, and even stuffed it back up into her chicken.

Two.

Janie Vivian declares an apocalypse while standing on a pile of rocks that has no significance whatsoever. This one is not rescheduled. This one is not miscalculated. This one is true. It's true. It's true. It's true.

One—

"Micah!"

A car door slams and Dewey is running, but I'm on the last match, and he stops. His hands are high. "Micah," he says, calm now. Forced calm. Full of pressure. "Micah, you look like shit."

The last match is in my hand. The ice is thin and bright under my feet. I hold the head against the lighting strip. Press it down.

"I feel like shit, honestly," I tell him.

"I figured," he says. Slowly. He talks slowly. He moves toward me slowly and stops at the edge of the quarry. Puts one foot onto the ice.

I don't want slow. I want a flick of the wrist. I want to drop. I want this to be over.

"I killed her," I tell him matter-of-factly.

And I flick my wrist

And the match comes to life

And I'm about to throw it down

And follow

When Dewey says,

"I did, too."

And the match

burns.

"What?"

"She wrote on the rocks," he tells me. "She wrote the things people called her, horrible things. They found them, when they got the body out. You want to know how she died? That's how she died. She put rocks everywhere she could and she walked into the quarry. She wrote shit on them like *slut* and *whore* and they dragged her down."

I stare at him. He stares back. The moonlight is terrible and everywhere. Dewey takes a step onto the ice.

"I let her," I finally say. "Didn't I? I remember. I told her we should stop trying. After she kissed Ander. Even though Ander—even though he . . ."

I heard and I knew and I never asked her about it. I never tried because I didn't know how.

"Yeah," says Dewey. "You were shitty. You were a shitty friend."

"And Ander," I say. "Nothing's going to happen to Ander?"

Dewey is quiet for a moment. "No," he says finally. "I don't think so. I mean, you know. No one can do anything now. Maybe her parents, but fuck them."

The match burns lower

lower

toward my fingers.

"He's going to get away with it," I say, "and I was a shitty friend."

"And she was a manipulative bitch. And I chain-smoke and never gave her a chance. And neither did anyone else."

"Apocalypse," I say. My lips make the shape but I can't hear the words. I stare and stare at the match. "Entropy. I just want it to be over. I just want it all to end. Okay?"

"Why the fuck would you want that?" he asks.

I blink. I look up at him, and he stares back.

"I let her go," I say, and I hear it this time. More. Her blurry voice behind me. Her breath catching and never coming out when she didn't answer my questions and I didn't ask again. Her heartbeat in her fingertips and her fingers around my wrist and her nails digging into my palm.

He takes another step. "Yeah, we've gone over that. You were shitty. I was shitty. She was shitty."

"It's all going to shit. So it should all just end."

The ice is bright with moonlight under my feet and all I

can think of is Janie under it. Walking into the water with her pockets full of stones.

The fire is at my fingertips and it begins to burn.

But then somehow Dewey's there, and his hand is on my elbow, and he's pulling me away onto solid ground, and the match

the match it slips

and falls

not onto the ice

but onto the rocks

where Dewey steps on it.

He looks at me hard in the eyes and says, "Well, that's stupid."

My hand is empty. No fire. No digging nails. "Huh?"

"Just be a better friend, you idiot."

There is no imbalance this time. It's not the earth that tilts; finally, it's just me.

I wake up on the ground with rocks digging into my cheek and a match beside my face. My glasses are cracked again, but the world is rebuilding itself and Dewey is talking fast into the phone to what sounds like my dad.

I wait for them to finish, and clear my throat. Dewey comes over. He crouches beside me, elbows on his knees.

I look at him and say, "There was this thing she wanted

to do. Well, there were a lot of things she wanted to do. But there was this trip to Nepal, this volunteer trip, for women's rights."

"Okay," says Dewey.

"I bought her a plane ticket for our birthday," I say. "I think I'm going to use it. I'm going to go."

"Okay."

"You want to come with me?"

He looks at me for a moment, a moment passing. And he nods. And I nod. And then I reach into my pocket for Janie's rock, and stare at it. Maybe I'll give it to Piper. I no longer need the reminder. There is nothing left to remember.

I am not afraid.

Also by
AMY ZHANG

An icy road. A girl. An end, or a beginning?

Falling into Place

AMY ZHANG

Greenwillow Books
An Imprint of HarperCollins*Publishers*

www.epicreads.com